BY THE LIGHT
OF THE COAL OIL LAMP

MEMORIES OF A SMALL-TOWN
SASKATCHEWAN CHILDHOOD

RUTH WOODWARD-CAMERON

 FriesenPress

One Printers Way
Altona, MB R0G 0B0
Canada

www.friesenpress.com

ISBN
978-1-03-911555-2 (Hardcover)
978-1-03-911554-5 (Paperback)
978-1-03-911556-9 (eBook)

1. Biography & Autobiography, Personal Memoirs

Distributed to the trade by The Ingram Book Company

Table of Contents

I would like to thank all of those people, adults and children, who lived in Garrick in the 1940s, who made my stories possible. I would also like to thank the Scott family, particularly Don and Denny Scott and Don's wife, Ruth, who were so hospitable when I visited Garrick in 2013. Most of the town I once knew was gone. I also want to thank their sister-in-law, Ellen Scott, who grew up as a member of the Lewis family and is unfortunately, now deceased. She organized a committee which produced a book called "From Forest to Farmland: A History of Garrick and District", which begins in the 1920s and is full of pictures and information about the town. My mother, Nena Woodward, ordered a copy from friends in Garrick when she lived in Winnipeg after 1950, and I still have the book.

My grandparents all came to Saskatchewan in the late 19th and early 20th century. I know that because, when I was a little girl, I heard grown-up people saying that governments were giving free land to people who would come and farm in Canada. Some of them said they were afraid that the United States would come and take over Canada if we didn't get lots of people from Canada living and farming on the prairies.

My parents, my Mommy and Daddy got married in Yorkton, Saskatchewan in 1938. Daddy told me later that he was born in 1912 in a little Saskatchewan town called Strongfield. Grannie and Grampa Woodward got married in England, and then Grampa came to Canada to find a job and a place for them to live. After that he wrote a letter to Grannie and told her how to come to Strongfield. Daddy was the oldest boy of their family of seven children born in Strongfield.

Mommy's family came from Russia. I called them Babba and Dedda. Babba was a name that was short for Babushka, and Mommy told me it was the Russian name for a grandmother. Dedda was short for Deddushka, and that was the Russian name for a grandfather. Babba said she was just eleven years old when she came to Canada. Her family was named Maloff, and she did grow up on a farm in Saskatchewan. She later married Dedda, whose family was named Katelnikoff. He said he had come to Canada with his cousin when he was already a young man. They lived in Yorkton, Saskatchewan. Mommy was born there in 1913, the second of four children.

I thought I was a lucky little girl to have two grandparents called Grannie and Grampa and two other grandparents called Babba and Dedda. Some kids had to take a lot of time saying things like "Grannie and Grampa Mitchell" or "Grannie and Grampa Rutherford". But I didn't have to get my grandparents mixed up.

When Daddy finished high school in Strongfield, he went to Regina to study bookkeeping. Then he got a job in Yorkton at a company called Smith Fruit. He told me that he met Mommy at a dance. "I saw her, and I thought she was the sweetest little person I ever saw", was what he said to me when I was a little bit older. When they were first married they lived next door to Babba and Dedda in a house that Dedda had built on Myrtle Avenue in Yorkton. They told me that they had decided to get married on the Friday before a long weekend. Because of that they could take the bus to Saskatoon and spend their honeymoon on the long weekend in a big hotel called the Bessborough.

When I was much older, I realized that, to them, this weekend honeymoon was a luxury. It was 1938, the Depression of the 1930s was not yet over. But my Daddy did have a job, and his father had a job in Strongfield. My Mommy's father, not only had a job, but it involved his own ambitious business of building houses and selling and renting them to other people. Also he succeeded at this even though there were other people in Canada at that time who objected to non-English immigrants, who called them names, even insulted or made fun of them. Yet all of those people, good, bad, in the middle, were able to create a Canada where they could prosper, or at least survive, even a Depression. The Americans did not move north of the border.

My family were not wealthy, but my story will tell of a happy childhood among other good energetic people who settled the prairies. I didn't hear them brag about how they were rich or important. But they worked hard, often helped their neighbors, even those they didn't greatly admire, and they created a country where this little girl would not have to spend her entire life in the light of a coal-oil lamp. Our little girl shall take us on a journey through a childhood on the Canadian prairies that speaks to our achieving the future of our great country.

As we return to talking about the Woodward and Katelnikoff families, my Mommy and Daddy, I will have to tell you I was born in Ontario. But my story is still about the prairies of Saskatchewan. And here it begins.

My Street in Fort Frances

Our house in Fort Frances had a front porch with screens along the front and sides. There was a cement sidewalk along the street, and a gate opening into the front yard. After you opened the gate you walked along our sidewalk and up the steps to the porch door. Across the porch was the front door that went into the living room. I was standing on the front porch, and I had a problem. I was wearing a harness. I knew why Mommy had put me in the harness. I started walking since January, and my first birthday was in March. When it was still cold outside I was happy to run around inside the house. Now it was July, and it was warm outside. There was sunshine, and it was so much fun to run around on that grass that grew beside the sidewalk. I loved running. I heard Mommy tell her friend, Mrs. Fedorchuck, that I was "very active". Then one day I found out I could reach that round thing on the front gate. I pulled down on it. I ran out onto the sidewalk. I was surprised. I just stood there for a minute, and it was then that Mommy came running out of the porch. She rushed onto the sidewalk and pulled me into her arms.

"Oh, you scared me," she said. I heard her say to herself, "What if she runs out into the road? She could get run over by a car. Oh my God."

We went back into the house. It was cooler and not as bright and sunny in the living room. I went to go back onto the porch, but the door was locked. Mommy picked me up and started talking to me. I think she was telling me that I could not go out onto the porch. But I didn't like that. It was nice out there.

She must have thought of something because the next day Daddy came home from his job downtown with this harness thing. It was made out of leather straps that fit over my shoulders and around my tummy. A long piece at the back was hooked onto a big round loop that Daddy nailed onto the wall of the front porch.

Two leather straps across my stomach were held together by a big safety pin. The first day I was on the porch in this harness, I did not like it. I couldn't even run to the end of the porch. I didn't like that. I wanted to run around. Ever since I ran out of the porch, I wanted to do that again. One summer day on the porch, I was thinking about how I was going to open the safety pin. I knew how a safety pin worked. I had seen Mommy doing up my diapers with one. I wanted to get out of that harness.

Suddenly I got what I wanted. The pin sprang open. It hurt. Then I was staring down at my thumb. It had a red line running down the middle of it. What happened to my thumb? There was a red line of blood running down the middle of it. I never saw anything like that before.

I started yelling, and Mommy ran out of the living room onto the porch She undid the harness and took me inside. She sat me down on the toilet seat in the bathroom, and got some things out of the cupboard up on the wall. She put something from a bottle on my thumb. It hurt. Then she put a bandage over the part where the blood was. "It's not too serious, Ruthie," she said. I jumped off the toilet seat and started to run back outside to the porch.

"No," said Mommy. "That has not been going very well. You can stay inside now." She went and got my dolls. I played with them on the kitchen floor while she made supper.

She let me go out onto the front porch the next day. But the harness was not tied around me any more. It was tied around the latch on the door between the front porch and the steps down to the sidewalk.

Sometimes in Fort Frances, Mommy would take me for a walk down the street to visit her friend, Mrs. Fedorchuck. That was fun because Darya was Mrs. Fedorchuck's daughter and she was my age. We could play together in the yard or in their house. Then our Mommies would pour themselves cups of coffee and sit and talk. Sometimes I didn't understand what they were talking about, but I thought maybe I wasn't big enough yet to know all the words. Then one night Daddy was talking, and he laughed and said to Mommy, "So were you and Nadya Fedorchuck talking in Russian or English today?"

"Oh, Bert," said Mommy, "You know Nadya is Ukrainian and that is not the exact same as Russian. Everybody back in Saskatchewan knows that. Even people from England, like your Mom and Dad. But we can talk in both languages. We're smart you know." Then they gave each other a big hug.

Well, I knew that Mommy and Daddy had both grown up in Saskatchewan, and then they got married in a town called Yorkton. Then there was something called the "Depression." Grown-ups needed money, so Daddy found a job working for a company called Smith Fruit, and they moved to this town called Fort Frances in this province called Ontario, and that's where we were now. I knew they missed their families, and they phoned them sometimes, but I heard them talk about how phoning cost money. I think with adults that "costing money" was not a good thing.

My Baby Brother

Then one day a big thing happened. Mommy went to the hospital. I was scared when Daddy took me over to Mrs. Fedorchuck's house before he went to work in the morning. But he told me not to be scared, and he said that I had a nice surprise coming.

Then Mommy came home with a baby. She told me he was my new little brother, Peter. I was in my crib in my own bedroom, but Mommy put Peter to sleep in the big bedroom with her and Daddy. He had his own little bed in the basket that she called the "wicker basket". It was the basket where she used to take the wet clothes from the washing machine out on to the back steps to hang on the clothesline. Now it was baby Peter's own little bed with his own little blankets.

One day, soon after they came home from the hospital, she unwrapped him from his blankets and laid him on the table to change his diaper. I remembered diapers, but I didn't wear them any more. I was a big girl. I was already "two-and-a-half", as Mommy said. I wore pants, and if I had to pee or poop, I went and sat in my little chair, next to the grown-up's toilet in the bathroom.

Mom took off Peter's diaper, and then I was surprised. Between his legs, he had this funny little round thing. I didn't have one of those. I asked Mommy what it was.

She laughed. "Oh, Ruthie," she said, "I told you that Peter was a boy." I remembered that she had said that. I knew that I was a girl and that we were different from boys. But I had never seen any boys with one of these.

"Boys use this to pee with," Mommy told me. "We ladies and girls don't have them."

"What is it called?" I asked.

Mommy laughed again. "Well, when I was in nursing, we called it a penis," she said, "but many people call it a dinky. You can call it that."

So my little brother was a boy with a dinky. He was also different from me because he couldn't talk. Mommy said he would learn later when he grew bigger.

He started to grow a little bigger. One day, in the winter, Daddy brought out the swing seat and hung it in the living room. I remembered sitting in that seat, but I was too big for it now. It was made of heavy cloth, with a piece of wire around it, so that you could put both legs through the holes in the front and sit against the back part like sitting in a chair. It was hanging on some ropes attached to the ceiling. Mommy and Daddy sometimes pushed Peter back and forth in it, but they told me not to do that because I might push too hard or too fast and he might get scared.

But one night it was me who got a little bit scared. Peter was sitting in the swing seat, and I was standing beside it. Some light was coming in from the window next to the fireplace, behind the swing seat. Not much light was coming in because it was getting dark outside. I was afraid to move, I was afraid it would get darker. I was afraid in the dark, and it was so quiet.

But before it got much darker and quieter, Mommy opened the door off the porch and came into the living room. She dropped her shopping bags on the floor, and ran over to the swing. She pulled Peter out of the swing and sat on the floor with both of us held in a big hug.

"Oh, Ruthie," she said, "I'm so sorry. There was a long line-up at the store. I know you're afraid of the dark. And, Petey, you're so small." And she hugged us both some more. After that she even let me push Petey in the swing sometimes, but we were never alone in the dark again.

Bears and Back Steps

I was afraid of bears too. Why? The three bears in the story Daddy read to me, Mama, Papa and Baby Bear were nice, like people. Sometimes I heard grown-up men talk about shooting bears in the forest and bush outside of Fort Frances. They said those bears were "dangerous" and "vicious". But I never saw any of those bears.

The most scarey bears happened in my dreams. They were big and black and stood up and growled and raised their front legs with their claws pointing toward me. I was very afraid. One night was very scarey. Daddy must have been sleeping too. I woke up and shouted.

"Daddy, there's a bear in my room," I called out.

I heard him run out of his bedroom and right across the living room. Then I heard him bump into the fireplace before he turned and ran into my room. Maybe he hurt himself, but he picked me up out of my bed and hugged me.

"It's all right, Ruthie. See. There's no bear here. Just your room. Everything is all right."

Then he turned on my bedroom light and tucked me back into my crib I think he talked to me until I fell asleep.

When I got a little older, Mommy told me that I called out about the bear in my room quite often. But she only remembered the one time that Daddy was so scared for me that he woke up and charged out of their room in such a hurry that he banged into the fireplace.

Our house in Fort Frances also had a back yard with trees and a garden. When you went out of the back door from the kitchen, there was a board platform with a little fence around it, then wooden steps going down into the yard. One day I was playing in the back yard. Daddy came out of the house, and he start nailing a piece of metal onto the top of the steps. He told me it was called a "shoe scraper". There was mud on the bottoms of my shoes, and so he showed me how to rub each foot across the top of the scraper. The mud came off my shoes and onto the side of the scraper.

"So there you see, Ruthie," Daddy said, "if you get mud on your shoes in the garden at the back here, you can scrape it off before you come into the kitchen." I liked that idea. I practiced it a few times while Daddy and I stood there. I liked it so much that I always cleaned my shoes on the scraper before I went in. Sometimes I even scraped my shoes just for fun.

My Window in Summertime

When I was three we moved to Strasbourg, a small town in Saskatchewan. I remember getting there. We were traveling at night. There were lights on in the train car, and I stood in the doorway looking down the aisle between the seats. Then I looked up. In the glow of dim light, it seemed so, so high up to the ceiling of the railway car.

After we arrived in Strasbourg, Daddy ran the town Co-op store, and we lived above the store. That is the first time I remember sleeping in my "real" bed, when my brother, Peter, was moved into the crib. My bed was smaller than Mommy and Daddy's bed, but it didn't have sides like a crib. I could get in and out of it just like a grown-up bed.

But when summer came, there was a problem. My bed was under the bedroom window and the bedroom was above the front of the store. I was only three years old, so Mommy wouldn't let me stay up late.

As the summer evenings got longer, it was just not dark enough for sleeping. It was noisy too. I could hear people walking and talking on the sidewalk down below. Sometimes there were only one or two people, and other times there would be a big group. When it got later some of them might be shouting or arguing. Sometimes a car or a team of horses pulling a wagon went by.

I told Mommy about it, so she got some curtain rods, and sewed a pair of curtains that I could pull across the window to keep the sunshine out. The truth was, though, that I did not want to keep any of it out. I would get on my knees on my bed, lean my elbows on the window ledge and watch what was going on down on the sidewalk and the road below me.

The early summer evenings were filled with sunshine, and I was very, very interested in the people walking by on the street. Some of them were like my parents, older people than me. But some of the others were not much older than I was, or they they were kids who were already in school. Some were laughing and talking. Some others sounded rough, and maybe they were even swearing or shouting at each other. I heard things I had never heard before. I did not get to sleep early any time during that summer.

Daddy liked books and reading. Maybe he bought me this book that summer or maybe years later. But it was a book called "A Child's Garden of Verses", and in it was a poem by Robert Louis Stevenson called "Bed in Summer". Part of it goes like this:

> In winter I get up at night
> And dress by yellow candle-light
> In summer, quite the other way
> I have to go to bed by day.
>
> I have to go to bed and see
> The birds still hopping on the tree
> Or hear the grown-up people's feet
> Still going past me on the street.

So now I knew that I was not the only child who ever had this summer evening experience.

Up Above the Store

In one corner of our kitchen in Strasbourg there was a round hole in the floor. Mom told me that it was there because there used to be a chimney pipe from the store downstairs to upstairs where our kitchen was now. If I looked down the hole, I could see the counter at the back of Daddy's store where the butcher sold meat.

The butcher's name was Eric. He was a tall skinny man, and he had one of those accents that people who came from England had sometimes. I would call down through the hole, "Hi Eric", and he would sometimes call back, "Hi Ruthie". That was if he wasn't busy cutting up meat for a customer. Eric and Daddy both told me not to call down to Eric if he was busy with a customer.

Daddy in front of his store in Strasbourg

Sometimes I just liked to look at the meat if he brought it out of the freezer where he kept it in the ice. There were big pieces of red meat that he said were "beef" or "steaks". At times, when I was down in the store, and when he was not busy, he would answer my questions about some of the big pieces of meat. The big red beef pieces were from cows. There was another meat that came in pieces that were also pretty big before he cut them into smaller pieces for the customers. These were called "pork", and Eric told me that pork meat came from pigs.

He also had chickens. Sometimes we had one that Mommy cooked for Sunday supper. But the chickens were not pieces of meat like the beef and pork. They looked like real chickens, but somebody had cut their heads off. When Mommy cooked them, she would pull off all the feathers. Then she would stick her hand into one end of the chicken. She would pull out a messy handful of blood and other pieces that she told me came from inside the chicken's stomach. I sure didn't want to help Mommy do that.

The Dining Room Furniture

Tommy was a friend of mine in Strasbourg. One summer morning we were sitting at the bottom of the wooden steps behind the Co-op store. Our house was above the store, at the top of the steps. A truck turned into the lane and stopped right in front of us.

The driver got out of the truck and said, "Where's Mr. Woodward?"

"That's my Daddy," I said, "He's in the store."

"Okay. I guess I'll have to go round to the front," the man said, and he walked to the corner of the lane and turned into the street.

"What does he want?" Tommy said.

"I don't know." I answered. "Let's go and see."

"But we can be faster," I said, and I started up the steps and then went into the kitchen. Petey was playing with his toy trucks on the floor, and Mommy was cooking something on the stove.

"There's a man with a big truck downstairs, and he's going to see Daddy in the store," I said, as Tommy and I ran out through the kitchen and started down the stairs to the sidewalk beside the store.

"I'm so glad they're here," said Mommy as we ran down the stairs. "Tell Daddy I'll be down as soon as I finish this borsch."

We got to the front door of the store just as the man from the truck came around the corner. "My Daddy's right in here." I told him. I opened the door of the store and ran inside.

"There's a man with a truck in the back lane," I shouted to Daddy as I ran up to the counter. There was a lady standing in front of the counter and Daddy was putting some groceries into a brown bag for her.

"Just a minute, Ruthie," he said. "I have to finish with Mrs. Johnson's groceries."

"Are you expecting a delivery, Bert?" said the lady in front of the counter.

'Yes, Helen, we are," said Daddy. "We ordered a set of dining room furniture from the catalogue."

"That's what you're getting, Mr. Woodward, if that's your right name," said the man from the truck, as he walked up behind me to Daddy's counter.

"That's my name all right. Just give me a minute here," said Daddy as he finished filling Mrs. Johnson's bag.

"That sounds really good," said the lady at the counter, as she handed Daddy some money. "Does it have the padded chairs? What colour?"

As Daddy took her money and opened the cash register on his counter, he said, "We ordered the padded chairs. I think Nena wanted green. I've got to go and see."

"I'll be waiting round the back," said the truck driver as he walked back out of the store.

"Hey, Eric, can you watch the counter. My new furniture is here," Daddy called to the back of the store.

"Sure, Bert," said Eric. He wiped his hands on his towel and started coming to the front counter. Tommy and I ran out onto the street behind Daddy. When he and the man with the truck got to the back, Mommy and Petey were coming down the stairs. We all stood in the back lane and watched them unload things from the truck and carry them up the stairs.

The first piece was dark brown wood with shiny varnish on it and two sides like half a circle. "That's the tabletop," said Mommy. "The two sides can be pulled up. We will be eating at a round table. I love the colour of the wood." She was very excited.

When they came back down the stairs, Daddy and the truck driver took up a piece with two long curved ends sticking out. "Those are the table legs," Mommy said to us.

They brought the four chairs out last. "They really do have green cloth seats," I said to Mommy.

"They're beautiful," she said. "Just what I wanted."

The green material on the chairs seats wasn't soft like velvet, it looked sort of like some knitted sweaters, and it had copper-coloured nails holding it on to the seats.

Mommy and Petey and Tommy and I followed Daddy and the truck driver up the stairs. When we got up, they had the chairs in the front room and were putting the two pieces of the table together. The front room was next to mine and Petey's bedroom. Part of the floor was over the stairs that went down to the sidewalk in front of the store, and it had a window that looked out over the street just like my bedroom window did. One of the chairs was in front of the window, but the sun still shone on the table.

"It's perfect," said Mommy. "I know it's important to have a dining room table for Sunday suppers, and I'm so glad we have one now. But I'm going to make some buns to go with the borsch tonight, and we're going to have our supper on our new dining room table."

And that's what happened.

The End of that Big War

Connie Mae Oasten was a friend of mine in Strasbourg. Her younger sister was named Doreen. Daddy liked to joke with words, and he sometimes called her "Constance Mabel." Connie Mae didn't mind. She thought that name sounded funny, and she liked to say it over and over again. Then she and Daddy would both laugh.

She and Doreen lived down the street from our store in a house. They lived with their mother and their grandmother. I asked Connie Mae what happened to her father. She told me he was gone as a soldier to fight in the war. I had never heard of this war, so I asked my mother what it was about. She gave me quite a long story. She started by telling me that she and Daddy were "pacifists", and that meant they were people who did not believe that there should be wars. She said that Daddy was old enough that he did not have to join the army. So he didn't

"But remember Uncle Walter?" she said to me. Yes, I remembered my mother's brother from a visit to my Babba and Dedda in Yorkton. "Well," she continued, "Walter is younger than Daddy, and he was supposed to join the army. But he wouldn't. He told them that he was something called a "conscientious objector", and that he shouldn't be forced to go and fight against his religious principles. Mommy continued to explain to me. "The government didn't accept that. So your Uncle Walter is now detained in a camp for conscientious objectors up in northern Saskatchewan. There are some other Doukhobour men there. And some other men who belong to religions, some like the Doukhobours, that do not believe in war. There are also a lot of Japanese men. That is because Japan is one of the countries we are fighting against."

I wasn't sure that I understood all this, but I had heard about this war on the radio. It sounded as if a lot of people got killed, and I was glad that my Daddy wasn't one of them. Or Uncle Walter.

While we were still living in Strasbourg, this World War Two ended. Connie Mae's father came home. I heard from some other kids that their fathers had also come home from the war and also some other men in the town. One boy said his mother had been a nurse in the army.

Then I heard that we were going to have a parade in town to celebrate the end of the war. Well, that was exciting. One of my friends was decorating the wheels of his tricycle with coloured crepe paper. Then I found out that Connie Mae and Doreen were doing that too.

Mommy and Daddy talked about it before they said "yes" to me. I heard them talking again about being "pacifists" and whether they should let me celebrate war. Or anything to do with it. But it was a small town, and everybody was involved.

They finally agreed that I could decorate my tricycle. Daddy even had crepe paper in the store. I had fun picking out the colours and wrapping them through the spokes in my tricycle wheels.

One of the exciting things on the day was that Mr. Oasten was leading the parade. He was a very big grown-up, and he wore his army uniform as he marched down Main Street. He looked very tall and proud. Just behind him were the other men from town who had been in the war. The lady who had been the nurse was there too. There was a band playing, then everybody from the town was marching behind them cheering and singing. Connie Mae and Doreen were up ahead with the families whose fathers were in the front rows behind Mr. Oasten. Mommy and Daddy came too, and brought Petey with them. But I was not far behind.

The parade with all the singing and cheering kept moving until it reached the place in town where the two wooden sidewalks met and made a corner beside the road. There was a big empty lot there with a caragana hedge beside it, and a big brick house on the other side of the hedge.

When we got there we could see that the men in town must have put up some big wooden tables with benches beside them. Ladies were bringing pots and plates with bread and meat and salads and fruit on them.

Mommy came with a big bowl of macaroni and cheese, even if she didn't believe in war or war parades.

The picnic went on until after it got dark. Even after Mommy and Daddy took us home to bed, we could still hear singing and shouting. It was a very exciting day.

The Circus
on the Two-by-Fours

Petey and I were running through a field of tall grass laughing so hard. It was a summer day in Yorkton. Behind us Stevie was running and shouting, "Get out of here. And stay out, you stupid little brats. It's dangerous."

We kept running and kept laughing. Stevie turned around and went back to the house that he and Uncle Walter were building. Peter and I knew that Uncle Walter and Steve Yaholnitski had been friends since they were both boys in school in Yorkton. Now they were both in university in Manitoba. Walter was studying to be an architect and Stevie was going to be a dentist. But it was July now, and those big guys were out of school and home in Yorkton, just like Peter and I were here with our Mommy visiting Babba and Dedda.

Petey and I kept running through the grass, then across a dirt back lane and up the hill behind Babba and Dedda's house. As we climbed the back steps, we slowed down. We had to stop laughing and rushing. We didn't want Mommy to notice that we had been chased away from the new house again.

"Hi. Is dinner ready yet?" I said, with a big smile on my face, as we walked in. There was a pot boiling on the stove, but Mommy and Babba were both sitting at the kitchen table talking. I thought we had got away with it, but Mommy stood up and looked down at us.

"Ruthie," she said, "I heard Stevie yelling at you kids just now. Were you in that new house again? Were you walking on the two-by-fours? Or what were you doing?"

Peter and I both stared at the linoleum on the kitchen floor. I did lie to Mommy if I had done something I knew I was not supposed to. But I could only do it once. Somehow, when she said she really knew what I had done, I was ashamed. I couldn't keep on lying.

"Yes," I said, still staring at the floor.

"Look at me, please." said Mommy. She wasn't a very tall woman. I always heard her say she was "five foot, two". She had her brown hair curled with a Toni permanent that I had helped her put in, so to me she wasn't scarey looking. I also knew that she hardly ever hit us, like some kids' parents did, even when she did get mad. So I looked up at her and said, "Yes" again.

"Yes? What?" repeated Mommy. "I asked what you were doing."

"We were walking on the two-by-fours," I said, "like people do in the circus. Those people can do it. I never fall."

"I have told you before," said Mommy, "that that house is not a circus. It is a house being built. Those two-by-fours planks are there so they can lay a floor for the house over them. There is a concrete basement below them. I have told you many times before that if you fall, you will land on a cement floor. You could break your bones. You could die, sweetheart." She raised her voice at me. "And Peter is smaller than you. What if you made him fall? Your little brother."

I started to cry. "I'm so sorry. I would never want to hurt Petey. I forgot. I won't do it again."

Mommy leaned down and hugged me. "Please, Ruthie, don't do it again. It's very dangerous." My little brother pulled himself into Mommy's arms, and the three of us hugged, while I cried and promised never to play circus on a building site again. And I really meant it, and I think Mommy believed me. At least the first few times.

But it wasn't the last time I played circus performer on the two-by-fours over concrete basements. Petey was more careful and did it less often, but he still did it too.

Our House Along the Lane

When we first moved to Garrick, we lived in the old hotel on the main street. We could walk out the front steps and along the wooden sidewalk across from the hitching posts where people tied up their horses when they came into town. Maybe we were living there because Mommy wanted time to add a kitchen to our house. I remember hearing her say to Daddy, "We really need a kitchen, Bert."

I think they also talked about the house going along with Daddy's store because they were both on the same "lot". The store was on the big main street, and it was just sideways across the dirt lane from the post office. The postmaster lived in the back of the post office, just like Grannie and Grampa did in Strongfield. The Rutherford's house was behind the post office, and across on our side of the lane there was no other house, just our woodpile. It was full of big pieces of old trees dropped there from somebody who came into town with a truck. Daddy had an old tree stump there for a chopping block. He kept his axe in the porch of our house. Then sometimes when we needed wood for the stove, he would go out and chop the big pieces of old trees into smaller pieces. Then he took the smaller pieces up to the house to put into the stoves. He had to chop a lot more wood in the cold winter days than in the summer.

Across the path from the woodpile was our toilet. Some people called a toilet an "outhouse". I heard Mr. Rutherford once say that outhouse was a show-off word. "A shit-house is a shit-house," he said. I didn't think kids were supposed to say that word.

Our house in Garrick – Faye, Ruth, Peter, baby Polly in her basket

To get to our house from the woodpile and the toilet, we walked along a path through a bunch of poplar trees. I loved poplar trees. If there was a little bit of wind on a sunny summer day, the little leaves of the poplar trees looked like they were shivering back and forth. Across from our poplar trees was the back of Mr. Drumheller's butcher shop and the big shed where he kept ice to keep the meat cold.

Our house was the last house on the corner where the lane met the next town road. That was a gravel road that ran from the corner where one of the town wells was, then across to the corner beside Mr. Schindel's field next to the road where we walked up to school.

Well, maybe before there was a kitchen, our house only had three rooms. There was the big room that we called the "living room." The round stove was there and the chesterfield and the piano, and the little table under the window that the radio sat on.

Under the other window that looked out onto the road, we had the table and chairs where we ate Sunday supper.

On one side of the round stove was the door into Mommy and Daddy's bedroom. They had a dresser for clothes and a window that looked out into the side yard. That was where our swing and Mommy's clothesline was.

On the other side of the round stove was the door into the bedroom that Petey and I shared. We had a bunk bed, and I got to sleep on the top bunk because I was the oldest. The bunk bed had a ladder at one end for me to climb up to the top. Behind our door was the toilet. Mommy called it "the indoor toilet."

Our window looked out at the back yard, so I could see the poplar trees. Under the window Mommy had put an orange crate that she got from Daddy's store. It was wood, and it had two parts where the oranges were packed when Daddy got them off the train. When he put the oranges out to sell in the store, the empty wooden box was there to stand up on its end in our bedroom. The bottom half was Petey's cupboard to put his toys in or whatever he wanted or what Mommy told him to put there. The top half was mine, and I put some things on the very top too, just under the window. We had another orange crate too, lying on the floor across from the bunk bed. That was where Mommy put our clothes. Mine were in one side and Petey's on the other side.

When they finished adding the kitchen to the house, we could walk right out of the kitchen into the living room and back again. The row of kitchen cupboards that looked out onto the back lane and Mr. Convoroy's back yard were below a window ledge where Mommy kept her plant pots with red geraniums in them. Sometimes she had other flowers there too. On the floor beside the cupboards was the stool where Daddy shaved in the morning with water from the pail of water he kept on the cupboard shelf.

Across from the cupboards was our great big kitchen stove. It was a lot bigger than the round stove in the front room, and it had a big flat top so Mommy could put pans of food to cook on it. It had four lids on it that Mommy and Daddy could open with the metal handle to put more wood in. Sometimes they just opened the lids because they wanted to check the fire, but we kids weren't allowed to do that. There was a cistern at the end of the stove near the living room door. Daddy always kept the cistern full of water, and if the stove was on, the water was hot. Then Mommy could use it for washing things. The dishes always needed washing, but maybe something else needed cleaning too.

Our kitchen table was in front of the kitchen window that looked out at the road. It was not as big as the living room table, and its chairs did not have soft padding on their seats. But I liked it anyway. I was allowed to sit in front of the window. On long summer days, we would have supper when the sun was still shining. I could feel it on the back of my neck, and I could see the shadows and the light on the kitchen floor and the fronts of the cupboards.

When we walked out the back door of the kitchen, we weren't outside yet, we were in the shed. It was full of stuff piled on the floor and on the shelves on one wall. There was Mommy's washing machine and a cardboard box where our gray cat, Misty, slept and where she kept her baby kittens when they were born. There were two big shovels and a rake and a hoe. When I got my bike, I kept it there if I wasn't out riding it.

After a while, Daddy got a bunch of flat rocks that he piled near the poplar trees. One Sunday in the summer, he took them all and dug up some dirt outside the porch door and laid all the rocks out in a big flat space. He said it was called a "patio". I liked it because when it rained a lot, it was not so muddy, and I could scrape off my shoes or my boots before I went into the house. In the winter Daddy shovelled the snow off the patio before he shovelled the path that went along through the polar trees, past the toilet and the woodpile and down beside his store and the wooden sidewalk in front of the store.

The Curtains on Fire

I remember one time in the winter, when I felt really scared, then really sad. I was helping Mommy clean up after supper. We were taking the dishes off the kitchen table and putting them in the dishpan to wash. We had some water boiling in a pot on the stove to put into the dishpan with enough soap to wash and dry the supper dishes. The coal oil lamp was still sitting on the table. We needed it for light when we had supper on a winter evening. I wanted to move the lamp over onto the counter so we could get everything off the kitchen table. I put my hands around the glass part at the the bottom of the lamp, the part where the coal oil was. Then something awful happened. There were still dessert dishes on the table so I moved the lamp closer to the side of the table near the window. The hot glass at the top of the lamp must have brushed against one of the the kitchen curtains. Suddenly the curtain was on fire. I screamed "Mommy". I was really scared. But Mommy was fast. She turned around. She grabbed the pail of water from the counter, the water that Daddy used to shave in the mornings. She rushed over and threw the water on the burning curtain. The fire was out. She missed the lamp. Even when I was so scared, I had put my hands around the bottom and moved it away from the burning curtain. We stood there for a minute. The bottom of the curtain was burned and black. The lamp was still burning as if nothing had happened. I started to cry. "What did I do?" I sobbed.

Mommy hugged me. "You didn't do it on purpose, Ruthie," she said. "It was an accident. But you must be more careful next time." Daddy and Petey came home from the store a little later. I was not crying by then, but

Daddy told me too that I must be more careful if I was doing anything with one of the lamps.

I was so sad the next day when I looked at the burnt black curtain. Then when Mommy took it down off the curtain rod, she said, " I have exactly the right piece of cloth left over from sewing that blouse last summer. The curtains will be shorter, but they will be nice and new." I was still ashamed, but not so sad any more.

Our Funny Neighbour

Across the lane from our house was the fence that Mr. Converoy built around his back yard. His door was facing onto the main street, but his back yard was full of grass and weeds because he hardly ever came out of his little house. And when he did come out, he sometimes waved a gun around as if he was going to shoot people. Some of the adults talked about that, but I heard them say a few times that he never had shot any real bullets. Or they might say he was "just a crazy old man."

But one day I heard the shooting and I climbed up onto our cupboard to look out the window to see if Mr. Convoroy was in his back yard. Daddy was home, and he came running out into the kitchen.

"Get down from there right now, Ruthie," he said. "Those shots might be real bullets, and you are right in the line of fire." He pulled me down off the cupboard and back on to the kitchen floor. No bullets came through our window, but I did not climb up there again when I heard the shots.

The Fire

Beside the old hotel, where we lived when we first moved to Garrick, there was a little house between the hotel and Daddy's store. It was just a little house with no upstairs. It had no front porch, but two little wooden steps went up to the front door. There was a window on each side of the door. It was not a fancy house, like the Schindel's brick house, but there were white lacy curtains inside both of the front windows.

Nobody lived in the little house, even when we first moved to town. When I was in grade one, Elaine told me that an old lady used to live there, but she died. Elaine said she remembered hearing her Mom say to Mrs. Drumheller that there was something they didn't like about two young guys, who said they were the lady's sons, coming into town and taking her body away. "They said they were going to bury her back in her home town," said Mrs. Drumheller. "I bet they were just trying to steal things from the house."

Then Elaine told me her Mom said, "But they had a key."

"Just a couple of crooks," was what Mrs. Drumheller answered.

After that nobody ever came back to the little house. It was empty.

Then, one sunny summer morning, someone started yelling, "Fire! Fire!" He was standing on the road in front of the little old house. Everybody in town came running.

Arty and I were playing near the railway station. We heard the shouting and saw everybody running. By the time we ran across the field from the railway station to the road, we saw lots of the men in town lining up across the road. One of the town wells was just across the street from my Daddy's store, a little closer to the empty old house.

Mr. Mitchell was pumping water from the well into a pail. Mr. Joseph picked up the pail of water. He ran across the road and threw the water onto the flames that were coming out of the front of the house.

"The house is on fire," Arty shouted at me, and we ran behind the well and over on to the road as his Dad came running up with another pail to fill with water. Mr. Smith came running up from the hotel, and Mr. Emde parked his dray down the road and came running with two pails. Daddy came running from his store with another two pails. Soon all the men in town were lined up in a row between the well on the field and the front of the house.

Mr. Mitchell kept pumping the pails full of water. The men passed them to each other along their row, across the road and the wooden sidewalk, until the man who was in front of the house threw his pail of water onto the flames. He passed it back to the man behind him. The empty pail got passed along the row of men and back to the pump. Then it got filled with water and passed back to be dumped on the burning house again. Lots of pails were getting passed along.

Us kids had all pushed ourselves together along the side of the hotel and the sidewalk in front of it. We all watched as the men passed pails of water back and forth and threw them on the fire.

It got very scarey, because the fire kept getting worse. I thought about the beautiful curtains burning inside. I heard the sound of breaking glass. I couldn't see the windows from where I was standing with Faye and Elaine, but I was sure the front windows had broken. Then I got very scared when the flames shot up out of the roof. The men were still pouring pails of water on the fire. The water was supposed to stop the fire.

I was jumping up and down. "Why is the fire getting bigger?" I shouted.

"Because it has to burn the whole house down, silly." Faye shouted from beside me.

"But the water is supposed to put it out. All our dads are putting so much water on it. They're passing the pails fast."

I looked again at the row of men moving the pails. Daddy was near the front of the row.

Just then I noticed a new flame shoot out from where the front door used to be. Some of the men near the front jumped away, so they were not so near to the moving flame. But they kept on passing the pails of water.

Then I saw that my Daddy was one of the men who had to jump out of the way .

"Daddy, Daddy, be careful," I couldn't help myself from shouting out.

"He can't hear you, silly. Let them keep stopping the fire," Faye shouted at me. We were all shouting now, there was also the noise of the flames, the men yelling about what to do next.

"But my Daddy's there. He might get hurt." I started to cry.

"Don't be such a crybaby. This is a big, bad fire. We have to be brave." Elaine was beside Faye now and looking at me instead of the fire.

"Sissy, crybaby," they both started yelling and laughing at me.

I looked again at Daddy and heard the shouting men and the loud sound of the flames that were all around the house now.

I cried even more. "Daddy, Daddy, don't get hurt." I was so scared.

All of a sudden Mommy was beside me. She told me later that she had gone away back down the lane and though our yard behind the house that was on fire. She had seen me crying and she was worried about me.

She knelt down beside me and put her arms around me. I heard Faye and Elaine whispering something. "Shut up, you two. Shut up and go away." said Mommy. They moved away. There was not much room to move because so many of us people were standing beside the wall of the hotel watching the fire.

By then the roar of the fire was starting to be more quiet. The roof had crashed down between the walls, and the walls of the little house were almost gone into the burning pile.

The men were still shouting and passing the pails of water from the well and onto the burning house.

"Is Daddy okay?" I turned to Mommy, still crying. "I'm afraid," I said, and as I saw my Daddy still in the line of men passing pails of water to each other, I started to cry again.

"Daddy will be fine, Ruthie. You stop crying now.", said Mommy as she hugged me next to her. "See. The fire is going down now. They've almost put it out."

I could see she was right, when I wiped my eyes and looked up. There were still flames, but mostly smoke now, coming from the place where the little house used to stand before the fire.

"I didn't know it had a cellar. Do you see that, Ruthie?" I knew she was trying to get me to stop crying. I looked over at the line of men. Daddy was still passing pails of water. Then I knew he was okay. He was not going to get burned or die.

I looked over to where Faye and Elaine were standing. Mr. Rutherford was still in the line of men passing pails of water. But they weren't looking at him. They were sticking out their tongues at me and waving their fingers.

I was still scared, but I wished they hadn't seen me crying. I knew they would keep making fun of me for being a sissy. But I really was scared about Daddy.

The fire soon died down, and nothing was left of the little old house but the ashes piled in the hole that was the old cellar. The men still stayed and poured more water and talked about how much they needed to be sure that no new fire started and nothing else went wrong.

And then later that day, when it was already afternoon, something else happened. Into town, over the railroad tracks, and down the road, came a black sort-of-a-truck, sort-of-a-car. The adults who were still standing on the road between the well and the burned-out house started yelling and laughing.

"What took them so long?"

"Who called the fire department?"

"Did you know we had a fire truck?"

It really did turn out to be a fire truck. Someone had made a call from the phone in the post office. They found out that somewhere in the district there was a fire department. It just wasn't very close. The adults laughed about this for days

And Faye and Elaine kept calling me a crybaby.

And Daddy was okay.

My Little Chickies

When we first moved to Garrick, we arrived one cold night in January, in the middle of winter. When spring came, Mommy and Daddy decided to buy some little chicks. I heard them talking about their plan to do what many farm families around our town did. They would raise their own animals for roast-chicken supper on Sunday. So Mommy and Daddy put up a little square wire chicken coop to keep the chicks safely in our back yard and brought home some bags of grain to feed them. There was also a small shed in our back yard. I think it had once been a dog house, with a pointed roof and an opening in the front for an animal to go into. Mommy said the chicks could run into it if it rained. Sometimes I saw them do that.

Mommy also said I could help her feed our new little pets. I would take a cupful of grain and throw it over the wire fence on to the dirt in the chicken coop. I liked watching the little chicks rush over in a crowd to peck away at the grain.

As spring wore on and headed for summer, I began to notice our little critters growing bigger. And some of them started acting differently than some of the others did. Some were pushy about grabbing the grain. Some were shy and stayed back. I thought these chickens were like some of us kids when we played together.

My Daddy liked to read to me and my brother at bedtime. He also ordered books from something called The Book of the Month Club. The books came to Garrick on the train with the mail. Some of them were books for grown-up people, but he also got two books for us. One was called Grimm's Fairy Tales and the other one was called Anderson's Fairy

Tales. I liked all the stories in the two books, but I especially liked the stories that had chickens in them.

These story-book chickens behaved like people, just like our chickens did. In the stories, they could talk like people. And they made friends with each other. They visited kings and princesses. I knew that a lot of these things they did were only stories, but I loved them anyway. And I loved to imagine the chickens in our back yard being like the ones in the fairy tales.

As summer came along, and they got bigger, I gave names to two of our chickens. Mommy said the lady chickens were hens, just like in the fairy tales. So I called one of the lady chickens "Henny Penny". One of them was growing bigger than the others. Mommy said he was a man, and that men chickens were called turkeys. So, just like in my fairy tales, I called him "Turkey Lurkey".

I was thinking of giving some of the other chickens names too. Mommy said that maybe two was enough. They were my special favorites.

All the chickens grew bigger during the summer. I still liked to feed them, and call my two special favorites over for some extra grain. But on one cool day in the fall, something happened. It was a Sunday when Mommy roasted a chicken and served it for supper with stuffing. It was a good supper, but I didn't think it had anything to do with my favorite backyard friends. The fall days got cooler, I had started school and forgot about the back yard for a while.

Then one Sunday, I walked through the back porch. Daddy was there beside a short tree stump with a flat top. He was holding a chicken in one hand and an axe in the other. As I stood there, he brought the axe down onto the chicken's neck. It's head, and a whole lot of blood fell onto the porch floor.

"What did you do?", I gasped. He turned with surprise and looked at me.

"Oh, Ruthie," he said, "I didn't see you there."

I started to cry. "Is it dead?", I said. Daddy sighed. Then he said out loud, "You are old enough to know. We bought these chickens to raise up, so we wouldn't have to spend money to buy them for Sunday supper. We do have to save money, you know. Remember that chicken we had last Sunday. Well, I had to kill that one too. Then you have seen Mommy cleaning out the insides and making stuffing, haven't you?"

I nodded, as I stopped sobbing and listened. "Yes", I answered.

"And don't you think chicken makes a good Sunday supper?", Dad asked.

I had to say "yes". That was true. But I did not like seeing that poor chicken's bloodied head on the floor.

Then I thought of something. "You won't cut the heads off of Henny Penny and Turkey Lurkey, will you?" I was almost shouting, not sobbing, when I asked that question.

Daddy frowned. "I know they are your favorites, Ruthie."

Then he leaned down and picked up the dead chicken and its head. "Let's get these into the kitchen, so Mommy can start making supper," he said.

Well, the fall weather got cooler, and Sunday supper was still chicken. And I did like chicken, and I did eat it. But I also went out into the back yard with handfuls of grain. And I called Henny Penny and Turkey Lurkey over too especially, so I could give them more grain than the other chickens.

The fall days got colder, and it started to snow. I still went outside, but I wore the new winter boots we had gone into Nipawin to buy, and I took special handfuls of grain to Henny Penny and Turkey Lurkey. By now there weren't many other chickens left.

Some Sundays we didn't have chicken for Sunday supper. Sometimes we might have other meat, but mostly baked potatoes or macaroni and boiled vegetables. Sometimes we had bread and milk, but that was more often during the week. Mommy said that was because milk was very healthy for our teeth.

But one snowy Sunday, the only chicken left was Henny Penny. And Turkey Lurkey was the only rooster. Mommy asked me to sit down at the kitchen table with her. She explained to me that food was expensive, and that meat was especially expensive. She knew that we all liked a special supper on Sunday, Daddy's day off from working in the store. She quietly asked if I agreed with that, and I said that I did. But I couldn't agree when she explained that she and Daddy had bought the chickens with the idea of raising them so we could eat them for supper. It was then that I started to cry. "But not Henny Penny and Turkey Lurkey", I sobbed. I don't remember the rest of our talk, but my parents were good people, and maybe my sobbing concerns were heard.

I don't remember eating Henny Penny. But I do remember, that as the winter wore on, and Christmas became closer, I would go out into the back yard to look at the little old dog house. It was usually covered with snow. But the top of it was covered with a blanket and some rugs from Daddy's store were hanging in front of the dog house's little door. Inside was Turkey Lurkey.

I don't remember eating him. Maybe it happened at Christmas dinner, or maybe before. What I do remember, in the next few years, was Mrs. Larson, who came into town from her family's farm every Saturday to sell chickens in Garrick. They were already dead and had their heads cut off. She would come into Daddy's store and he would often buy one for our Sunday supper.

Mommy and Daddy's Wedding

One of the first times we went on the train from Garrick was to visit Babba and Dedda in Yorkton. They lived on a street called Myrtle Avenue. Mommy told me that Dedda had built that house when she was a little girl, and that she had grown up there. There was another house next door, and she told me that Dedda had also built that house.

"Your Daddy and I lived there when we first got married. We were living here in Yorkton then. Daddy was working here."

"You got married here in Yorkton?" I asked.

"Yes." said Mommy. "We met here at a dance one night, and we started going out together. Then we got married at a civil ceremony. After that we came over here, to Babba and Dedda's house, and got together with a bunch of our friends and family to celebrate."

"What's a civil ceremony?" I asked.

"Well," said Mommy, "you know that Daddy and I don't go to church every Sunday like some people do."

"But I go to Sunday school sometimes. It's fun."

"I know you do, Ruthie," said Mommy. "Remember we all talked about that once. You can ask Daddy and me if you have any questions about the ideas of religion or God."

"I know that, Mommy," I said. But I wanted to know more about them getting married. "What's a civil ceremony?" I asked again.

"Well," said Mommy, "It's when you get married in front of a judge in a court house, not a minister in a church."

"Just the two of you alone?" I asked. I had seen pictures in magazines with ladies in long white dresses getting married in front of those windows with coloured glass pictures on them in big churches. Like maybe they have in the city.

"Not just us alone." said Mommy. "You have to have a witness."

I was just going to ask what was a witness, but Mommy started laughing. "We had something really funny happen at our wedding," she said. "Your Daddy's friend, Stephen, was supposed to come as his witness, but he didn't show up. We waited a little while. I think the judge was getting annoyed. And you remember, Ruthie, that I told you that Grannie Woodward, Daddy's mother, was here for our wedding."

"Oh, yes, I know Grannie was here then." I was a little scared of Daddy's mother. Grannie Woodward was a very strict lady. But she had told me about being at Mommy and Daddy's wedding.

"Well, Grannie was at the court house with us. She told the judge that she was Daddy's mother, but that she could be the witness if that was allowed. The judge said it was OK.

"So, you see," said Mom, still laughing, "the groom's mother was the witness when your Daddy and I got married." I didn't know much about people getting married, but I wasn't surprised that Grannie Woodward got it done.

"Then you came back here to Babba and Dedda's house for a party?" I asked.

"It was like a party," said Mom. "We had lots of good food and wedding cake with white icing. I cut the first slice because that's what the bride does. Daddy's sisters, Gwen and Louise, had both come to Yorkton on the train. Your Uncle Walter and Aunt Lydia were there, of course. So was Amy. She was my best friend in high school, and she still lived in Yorkton. Grampa Woodward couldn't come because he had to be at the post office in Strongfield. But two old friends of Babba and Dedda came."

"After that your Daddy and I left everybody and went to take the bus to Saskatoon. We had sent a telegram earlier and reserved two nights at the big hotel there called the Bessborough. That was our honeymoon. It was so exciting."

"But didn't Daddy have to go to work?" I asked.

"No." Mommy answered. "It was October 8, and that was Thanksgiving weekend. We decided on purpose to get married on that Friday because it was Thanksgiving and your Daddy had Monday off work. So we could have a long weekend for our honeymoon.

"That sounds like fun." I said.

"It was." said Mommy, and laughed.

She said they lived in the house next door before Daddy got moved to work in Fort Frances. Now strangers lived in the house next door. Mommy said that they paid money to Dedda, called "rent", so that they could live there. Now when we visited, we stayed only in Babba and Dedda's house.

Santa Comes to Garrick

We always had a tree at Christmas time. I'm not sure where Daddy got the tree, but every year it was in the corner of the living room between the door of Mommy and Daddy's bedroom and the window that had the radio under it. When they put the tree up they moved the radio on its table right over next to the chesterfield.

The tree was in a metal thing that had four legs sticking out of it so it could stand on the floor. The legs were made of red metal, and Daddy had to get out his screwdriver to tighten the metal thing before he stood the tree up in the corner.

Then Mommy brought out the box of decorations from the porch. The first thing that went on the tree was the star on the very top. Daddy was the only one tall enough to reach up up and put it at the top of the tree trunk. The star was made out of shiny silver metal, but before he put it up, he gave us kids some pieces of tinsel and little coloured ribbons to wrap around the five points of the star.

Sometimes he had to get out the stepladder and then take a knife up to the top of the tree trunk to make it smaller and more pointy so the star would fit on top. But he always got it to the top so the tinsel could sparkle at us.

Then he came down and gave the box of tinsel to me and Petey so we could hang the rest of it on the tree. But first Mommy got out the box of decorations, so we could put them on the tree with the tinsel. Lots of them were glass balls hanging on the end of a loopy piece of thread, so we had to be very careful not to drop them. They might break if that happened. Mommy and Daddy helped us hang up the decorations near the top of the tree where we couldn't reach, but Petey and I got to hang up most of them. There were some decorations, too, that were made out of wood. We had Santa with his big white beard and his red suit painted on the wood. There were two wooden reindeer and a bluebird. We were careful hanging those two, even if they wouldn't break like the glass balls might. At Christmas time Daddy sold some decorations in his store, and every year Mommy and Daddy let us pick out one new Christmas decoration to hang on the tree. One year, when we were in Nipawin just before Christmas, they let us buy some decorations in a store there too. It was so much fun to see our tree sparkling in the corner of the living room.

It was as much fun to listen to the radio at Christmas time too. Before it was even Christmas Day, they would play songs like "Rudolph, the Red-Nosed Reindeer" and "Santa Clause is Coming to Town". They also had the songs that the adults called Christmas carols, like "Silent Night" and "Oh Come All Ye Faithful." We sang those songs at school before the Christmas holidays, and they sang them at church too.

On the night before Christmas Petey and I would get pins and hang out biggest winter socks on the arm of the chesterfield. After Polly was born, we hung out a sock for her too. The next morning we would find the stocking full of treats like candy and gum and maybe an apple and an orange. But we were most excited about the big present that Santa had left for us under the tree. In the days before Christmas, we had wrapped presents for each other, and Mommy and Daddy had wrapped presents to each other and to us. But Santa left his presents after we had all gone to sleep on Christmas Eve. It was so much fun opening our surprises. Later in the day, we might go and visit the Rutherfords or other friends, and then Mommy would make a turkey for supper and we would have a special dessert.

One thing about Christmas made me a little sad. The year I was in grade two, Faye and Elaine told me that Santa wasn't real. I went and asked Mommy and Daddy about that. They sat down with me, and they said that maybe I was old enough to learn that it was true. All of us people made up Santa because the story was so much fun. I was thinking about how much it was really fun, and I stopped being so sad.

The next Christmas, I decided that I should not be the only kid in the family to know that Santa was just made up, so I told Petey about it. He started crying. Then he yelled at me and said I was lying. He didn't believe me. He must have told Mommy because she took me into my room by myself the next day. She didn't yell at me or anything, but she said Petey was too young to know there was no Santa, so she had told him that he did not need to believe me. And she said I should not tell him again. So he still believed in Santa until he was bigger.

Daddy and the Grouchy Old Farmer

Daddy liked to tell stories about when he was young in Strongfield. He had a Hallowe'en story from his teenage years. There was a farm not far outside of town, and when that farmer came into town, the boys in high school thought he was kind of rude and not a nice person. Whenever they offered to do chores for him in exchange for some coins, he always just said "no" and maybe "forget it" or some worse words.

So late one October evening, after they collected "Hallowe'en apples" from neighbors, and it was dark, the boys walked out to his farm. They saw that the house was dark, there were no coal oil lamps burning anywhere, no animals making noises, no people finishing off their chores.

So they snuck around the back of the barn. They found the wagon that the farmer used when he traveled into town to buy something. Of course, the horse that pulled it was unhitched and in its stall in the barn.

So what the boys did was begin to take the two wheels off the wagon. They had planned for this and brought some tools. Then they found a ladder and carried the wagon up to the roof of the barn. Next they carried the two wagon wheels up. They attached the wheels back onto the wagon. Each wheel was on one side of he roof of the barn.

"So far, so good," laughed Daddy as he told the story. There was still no sound from the farm house or the barn. The boys knew they had not been discovered. They climbed down from the barn roof, put the ladder away and quietly began to sneak back into town. Once they looked back, and they could see, against the night sky, that the wagon was sitting on the peak of the barn roof.

The next day not one of the boys from high school said anything when the story went around town that the grouchy farmer had found his wagon neatly perched on his barn roof when he went out in the morning. The adults didn't ask them much about it, because none of them really liked the grouchy farmer either. So the boys' Hallowe'en trick had been a success! For them, but not the farmer.

Summer in Yorkton

The first house where we used to go and visit Babba and Dedda in Yorkton had a bedroom window looking out over the back yard. There was a barn there behind the house. It looked just like the barns they had on farms, even if this was a street in the city. Aunt Lydia still lived with Babba and Dedda, and she told me that they used to have a cow in the barn for milk, but they didn't have one any more. She said it used to be her job to take the cow in the morning and walk it out to a field on the edge of town. Later in the day, after school, she would go back to the field and walk the cow back to the barn behind the house.

Now there were only rabbits in the barn. They were small and fluffy and kept in a wire cage. Babba told me that she would comb the fluff off the rabbits' fur and add it to things that she was knitting. Mitts or sweaters for winter were warmer when rabbit fur was added to the wool, she told me.

On Myrtle Avenue, across from the row of houses, there was an empty field. It was full of grass, and it had some trees growing on it too. They were the small skinny trees with the little leaves that were kind of round. Later, when we lived in Garrick, we had the same trees. We called them poplar trees, but Mrs. Haig said she had looked them up in a book, and they were called "trembling aspen".

Whatever they were called, I loved climbing on them. It was easy to climb a tree. You grabbed the lower branches, then pulled your feet up the trunk to the next branch. It was like climbing some steps, only you had to hang onto the higher branches. Mommy didn't like me climbing trees. She said it was for boys to do. But she let me climb the trees across the street because she thought they were not so high that I could get hurt if I fell. I told her I wouldn't fall. I didn't like people saying there were things that only boys could do. Lots of those things were more fun. So I did them if I could. I never ever fell off of one of the trees on Myrtle Avenue.

Further down the street was another empty field. Mommy told me that when she was a little girl, there was a school on that yard. She had started going to school with her older sister, my Auntie Ruth, when she was just four. They walked down the street together. At that time everybody in Mommy's family spoke Russian. Mommy found out that when Ruth was at school, she spoke English. She had learned it in school. Ruth told her that the teacher had said that Mommy could come to grade one when she was four years old. The teacher would not teach her, but she could hear other kids speaking English. Then when she started grade one, she would know enough English to learn to read. She also told me the story that she said Auntie Ruth had told her later. It was that the teacher had asked what Mommy's name was. When she heard that it was a Russian name pronounced "Anuta", the teacher said, "That sounds like Annie. We already have five Annies in the class. I am going to call you Nena."

When she told me this story, I said to Mommy, "Weren't you mad that the teacher picked a name for you?"

"No." answered Mommy. I liked the name Nena then, and I've always liked it. The teacher was right. There are lots of Annies around. But not so many Nenas.

Another story I heard from that house on Myrtle Avenue was that when Auntie Ruth was in grade nine, she got a sickness called "pleurisy." She had to stay home from school, and Mommy said she remembered that, during the spring time, Ruth sat out on the front porch most of the time. When the school year ended, she hadn't written any tests or passed grade nine. Then, Mommy said that a doctor in the Yorkton Hospital, who was a friend of Dedda's, said that he would take her into the hospital and train her to be a nurse.

They didn't tell me what happened next. I heard the story when I was in the Yorkton Hospital to have my tonsils out in the summer that I was seven. Mommy was sitting beside my bed when the doctor came into the room. They knew each other, and started talking. The doctor asked how Ruth was doing. Mommy told him that she was still a nurse in California, and they went on talking. It was later when Mommy told me that he was the same doctor who had brought Auntie Ruth into the hospital, and began her nursing training.

"It was a lot harder to get into nursing training when I did it later in a hospital in Edmonton." Mommy told me.

The Big Hole in the Ground

If you walked across the field from the railway station to the hotel in Garrick, then kept walking straight down the second big gravel road, past the cafe and Charlie Fong's store, then you passed the corner where the second town water pump was. That was the pump Daddy usually went to for our water. If you kept walking along that road, past the Joseph's house, but not so far as the Thompson's farm, you would get to a place where there was a really big hole in the ground. In the summer, the hole had water at the bottom when it rained, and there were weeds growing all around the sides of the hole and on the ground beside it. There were a lot of yellow dandelions mixed in with all the other weeds.

Adults told us kids to be careful and not fall into the hole. We thought that was silly. We knew better than to fall into a hole in the ground, even a big hole! But some of the bigger boys did go down to the bottom and splashed around in the water. One day I saw some boys pulling up weeds and yelling and throwing them at each other.

In the winter, that was all much better. Soon the hole was full of snow. There was snow all over the ground at the top of it and lots of snow along the sides and bottom of the hole. The bigger boys ran up and down and packed the snow, so then we had a bunch of slides down the sides of the hole.

Our parents didn't tell us little kids that we couldn't slide down in the snow. So if the bigger boys weren't around, or if they let us, we could slide down to the bottom. It was so much fun. At first. It wasn't as much fun to climb up. Then, later in the winter, there was more snow, and the path up got stomped down almost like a stairway.

One winter somebody made some ice at the bottom of the hole. We could skate on it. But them Mommy told me that it was only the bigger kids who could skate at the bottom of the hole. I might slip and fall or hurt somebody else with my skate blade.

But I did have skates, real skates. Some kids only had skate blades. They strapped them on over their winter boots. But Mommy and Daddy let me get real skates. They had their own boots, with skate blades on the bottom of the boots. We ordered them from Eaton's catalogue in the fall when I was in grade two. They fit me when they came on the train, and the pair of big warm socks we got fit me too.

The Curling Rink

But Mommy still said I could only skate in the skating rink. The only skating rink in town was the one that all the adults called the the "curling rink". Well, skating there was sort of okay, but we kids could only skate in the curling rink when the men weren't curling there. Most of the days, the men were at work, but quite a lot of the time on Saturday and Sunday in the winter, they were curling.

The curling rink wasn't far behind the hole in the ground. But it was a real building with a roof. It had a great big piece of ice, sort of like an icey sidewalk, that went straight down the middle of the building. There were some rows of seats along the sides. One row was higher than the other row. Lots of people came to watch the curling, so everybody could see, even from the seats on the second row.

At one end of the rink there were some big circles drawn on the ice. The adults knew that this was how some men won the game and some men lost. The men stood behind a line at the end of the rink and slid the curling rock back and forth on the ice until they let it go and slide down to the big circles on the ice at the other end of the rink. They got more points if the rock stopped right in the middle of the circles. But all the curling rocks didn't stop in the middle. Some of them stopped even before they got to the circles.

The curling rocks were big and heavy. They weren't really rocks. They were big sort of round things with a handle that looked like it was made out of some kind of metal, but the rocks looked like they were made out of glass. Daddy laughed when I said that. I was standing beside him before any game was started, and he said to me, "See if you can pick one up."

I leaned over and grabbed the handle. The curling rock didn't move. "It is really heavy," I said to Daddy.

"Try both hands," he said.

So I pulled with both hands. The rock moved a bit, but it seemed even heavier than before. Daddy laughed. "That's why curling is for grown-ups, Ruthie," he said.

Then he grabbed the handle of the curling rock. He didn't even lift it up. He moved it back and forth across the ice, then he let it go and it slid down to the other end of the rink.

"See," he said, "I was trying to get it right into the middle of the circle." Then he laughed, and said, "But it didn't quite get there. I would get a better score the closer it got to the middle."

So then, when we came to watch curling, I knew what the men were trying to do to win a big score. Sometimes it was so cold in the curling rink that I wanted to go out and walk home. But it was fun if Daddy's team won.

Second Avenue South

Babba and Dedda's house in Yorkton on Second Avenue South was more modern than the house on Myrtle Avenue, the one that Mommy had grown up in. Uncle Walter had designed the new one when he went into architecture.

And then Dedda had built most of it. It had big new windows that filled most of the wall on one side of the living room. That was called a picture window. The new house didn't have a barn behind it, so Babba didn't have any more rabbits. But it had a garage on one side of the house and steps that went down into the basement from the garage.

It had a bonya in the basement, just like the old house on Myrtle Avenue. Mommy told me that "bonya" was a Russian word, and that for many people it was like their way of having a bath. Dedda had built it in its own small room in the basement. In the room was a small black stove with a chimney pipe that went out through the room's roof and connected with the furnace pipes in the rest of the basement. The floor of the bonya had nice coloured linoleum over the cement basement floor. Then there was a smaller step, then a bigger step so that people could get up and sit on a bench made out of wooden boards. The higher you sat, the hotter it got. To make the room hot, there were two pails in the bonya room. We kept them full of water and you threw the water on the hot stove. That filled the room with steam. Steam was what a bonya was about. That was the only place I ever sat in steam and then washed my arms and legs, then put more steamy warm water on them. It wasn't just a bath, it was fun. Babba and Dedda had to have a bonya, and I was always glad that they did. I really liked to sit up on the top bench and watch Mommy or Babba pour water on the little stove and fill the bonya room with hot steam. It was more fun than having a bath in the blue tub in our kitchen in Garrick. Mommy once told me that there was a country in Europe called Finland and those people had the same thing as a bonya, but in their language they called it a "sauna". I thought both words sounded a bit the same.

But this new house in Yorkton also had a bathroom on the main floor across the hallway from Aunt Lydia's bedroom. This was a bathroom like pictures in some of the catalogues I had seen. I think I also remembered that we had a bathroom like that in the house in Fort Frances. It had one of those big white tubs that you could fill up with water from taps, and a white sink on the wall with more taps. It also had one of those white toilets, like they had in hotels, the ones with a round seat that you could sit on to pee or poop and then a lid that you could close when you were finished. When you pulled the handle, water washed all the pee and poop away. Dedda told me that it all went into pipes, then down into something called sewers that were buried in the ground.

Babba's Trip to Canada

There was one thing that was the same as in the house on Myrtle Avenue, and that was Babba's long wooden settee with the carved back and arms Where you walked into the kitchen from the back yard, there was a little nook beside the stairway, across from the kitchen cupboards and the new electric stove and refrigerator. Sunlight came into the nook from a window in its wall. The settee sat under the window beside the kitchen table with chairs on the other side. It was all tucked into the cozy nook, and Babba would often sit there and knit or play her games of solitaire.

I walked into the kitchen one day when I was tired of playing outside. Babba was sitting at the kitchen table with her game of solitaire laid out in front of her. I sat down across from her. I grabbed a deck of cards off the windowsill and laid out my own game of solitaire.

"Mommy said to tell you that she will be picking up the blue wool from the Woolworth's store before she comes home this afternoon," I said.

"That's good. It's a good colour, Ruthie. Nice for winter mitts."

"Mommy really likes it too. They don't have it in Garrick. Not too many colours there."

"That doesn't matter. Nena likes to go to go shopping when she's here in Yorkton." We sat quietly for a while, each playing our own game of solitaire. Twice, Babba reached over and moved a card that I had missed. I didn't mind. She was better at the game that I was. But I did hope that, just maybe, someday, I could notice a card she had missed. Then I would tell her about it.

"You told me last time," I said, "that when you came from Russia, you came on a sailing ship. How old were you?"

"I was eleven," she said. "My father drove from our village to the sea. I never saw water like that before. So much water. Not like in the mountains. We left the wagon and the horses in the town when we went on the ship. I don't know where they went."

"Maybe Dedushka sold them," I said.

"The town was called Batumi. There were more people on the shore. They told us to wait for the ship. My sister and I went with the others. We were all afraid to go far from the ship. But there were piles of grain all along on the shore near the sea. We played there near the sea, banging our feet down hard, puffing dusty mounds. And laughing. Then they came and got us to get back on the ship."

She went on. "The sails on the ship were high up. Sometimes the wind blew them and they made noise. I was scared a little bit, but I liked it. We sailed for days, and then we stopped at a very big city on the shore. That city was famous, my father told us. It was called Constantinople. There was more water and some more big cities where the ship stopped. Then the big cities stopped and there was only water. And sky. It was a long, long time after that when we got to Canada. We sailed right across the Atlantic Ocean, Ruthie."

She stopped talking, and we went on playing solitaire, as we often did, if I wasn't playing outside on a Yorkton summer afternoon. And I still kept hoping that I would get a chance to move a card she had missed.

A Sad Happening
in a Good Family

In Garrick, Mr. Lewis had a garage. It was down the street from Daddy's store, at the corner with the road that went up past the school and down to the road that went to Nipawin. He had a big sign on the front of his garage and a lot of room where cars could park when he worked on them. I think he also sold stuff like big cans of oil and things that farmers needed to put on other machines like tractors.

If you walked up the road past the house on the corner of the next street, where the very old man and lady lived, you would get to the Lewis's house. It was painted white and it was two stories tall. I always liked Mrs. Lewis. Mommy called her Lina. She was a big lady, and she always said a nice big "hello" if I came over to visit the house or play with one of the kids. Sometimes I liked talking to Mrs. Lewis more than I liked playing with the kids. Tina was a little bit older than me, and then there was Mary, who was older than Tina.

The one who was my age was Eddy. Sometimes I would go out and play with him around town. But sometimes I wasn't sure that I liked him all that much. He was a big kid compared to some of the other boys in our class at school. He tried to act tough all the time, and sometimes, if we went out to play, he would throw rocks at people's houses. But he never pushed me or hit me. One time he told me that he had stolen some candy from Charlie Fong's store. I was afraid to steal anything. Mommy and Daddy told me it was a bad thing to do. But mostly I was afraid I would get caught and get in trouble. But when he told me that, it made me think Eddy was brave. Maybe strong, like a grown-up person.

Denny was the youngest brother, and we were friends. He wasn't much younger than me, and I wasn't scared if I went out to play with him. He never talked about stealing things. One day in winter, we were playing in a snowbank beside the road that ran beside my house. We were climbing over the snowbank and when he got to the top, I pushed him down to the other side. He started yelling that his face was cold and his eyes were full of snow.

I said, "You're OK. You're just being a big sissy." Then he said, "I'm not a sissy." and he started to cry. For a minute, I felt sorry for him, but I guess I changed my mind. I picked up another handful of snow and threw it in his face. He got up and started running back toward his house. I started to chase after him, but I really didn't want to hurt him, so I watched him run home, and then I went back to my house.

Later, after it was dark, I was at home in our kitchen. Mommy was making supper. There was a knock on the kitchen door. I went and opened it, and Eddie was standing there. "Why did you hit my brother?" he said loudly. I was scared. For a minute I couldn't think of anything to answer. So I slammed the door shut in his face. I was afraid that he might knock on the door again, or that Mommy would stop her cooking and ask me what was going on. But nothing happened.

We had supper, but when I went to bed that night I was still scared. I was thinking that if Eddy saw me outside, he would try to beat me up for hurting his brother. The next day, I tried to stay in the house, but Mommy told me to go out and play. I went over to see Faye and Elaine. When Mrs. Rutherford told us to go out and play, I talked them into going down to Ronnie's house, because it was a long way from the Lewis's house.

I didn't see Eddy for a few days, and the next time I saw him with a bunch of other boys, he didn't say anything to me about making Denny cry. Then later I saw Denny. He didn't say anything about me hurting him, so I didn't say anything either. We were all friends again. I wasn't scared any more.

But I felt really sorry for the kids in the Lewis family in the next summer. Their Dad, Roy Lewis, the man who owned the garage, died. I didn't see the whole family for quite a while. The adults said that they had gone back to Mr. Lewis's home town for his funeral. They also said that what he had done was "commit suicide". I had never heard of this before. I learned that it meant he had killed himself. When the adults talked about it, they said that because he fixed cars, he knew how to do this. From seeing people who drove cars, I knew that smoke came out of the back of the car when it was turned on and moving. It seemed that this smoke had something in it called carbon monoxide. If people breathed it in, it could kill them. When the adults were talking about Mr. Lewis dying, and they saw us kids listening, they would tell us to go away, but after a few days, I heard most of what they said about what happened. It seemed that Mr. Lewis had locked the doors of his garage, then he had taken a long tube that he used for something when he fixed cars. He had put this around the pipe that puffed the smoke out of the back of the car, then put it though the car window and shut the window most of the way. Then he had locked himself in the car and turned on the engine. It seems that the car then filled up with this carbon monoxide gas. Mr. Lewis breathed it in until he died.

I heard that he was dead when Mrs. Lewis found him. When it got really late and he didn't come home, she went to the garage to look for him. She found that the door was locked. She had to go back home to get a key that she kept in the house. He was dead in the car when she found him.

The adults talked about him dying for days. They all wondered why Mr. Lewis killed himself. Some said it had something to do with sex, that Mrs. Lewis was doing this with some other man. I heard Mr. Schindel laughing and saying, "Who would want her?" and a bunch of other men he was talking to started laughing. Some people said he was "going broke", because the garage didn't have enough business. I asked Mommy what she thought.

"I don't know, Ruthie," she said. "Nobody seems to know. He and Lina got along well enough. He was a little tough with her, but you know the family. They got along pretty well. Someone would have known if he was seeing some other woman. He didn't go out of town much either. And what will Lina do now to support those children? It's just sad."

Well, the adults soon stopped talking a lot about it, the family came back into town, and Mr. Lewis' brother, from the town they grew up in, came to live with the family and run the garage. I didn't push Denny or rub snow in his face any more because I felt sorry for him. And Eddy never did try and beat me up for making his brother cry.

Playing With Matches

The Sullivan family came to Garrick when our family was already living there. Denny was about my age, and he had a little sister.

I liked to play with him around town. Mommy liked most of the kids I knew, but I think she didn't like Denny.

"I don't think you should hang around with him, Ruthie. He's not a good boy. If he tells you to do something that is bad, don't do it. Come home and tell me."

Well, I wasn't going to be a tattletale, and I still played with Denny. But maybe Mommy was right. One day I was walking with him along the lane that went behind the hotel and the stores that ran along the big main street up to Charlie Fong's grocery store.

The toilet in the corner behind the hotel was tipped over. It had been lying there tipped over for a long time. Some bigger boys must have tipped it on one Hallowe'en night. Somebody told me once that the Smiths had never put the toilet back up. Instead they had put a modern toilet in its own room inside the hotel. That was so the men who were sitting and drinking in the beer parlor did not have to go outside if they had to pee.

Well, Denny and I were looking into the toilet hole. There were weeds growing all around it, but you could still see all the messy poop at the bottom. He moved a little closer to me, and I got scared all of a sudden, and moved further away from the hole. I thought maybe was going to push me into the toilet hole. And into the poop.

Then we started walking back toward the hotel. We were right behind the back wall of the hotel when Denny pulled a box of matches out of his pocket.

"What are you doing with matches?" I said. Playing with matches was something that none of us kids was allowed to do. Adults would maybe let the kids who were in high school do that, but they were always telling us that playing with matches was dangerous. Nobody's parents would give them a box of matches.

"I snuck them from the drawer when my Mum and Dad weren't looking," he said.

"That's stealing," I said.

"I don't care," said Denny.

There was a pile of dead leaves and junk against the wall. Denny lit a match and threw it into the pile. Then he lit another match and threw it in too. A flame came out of the pile of leaves. Just then a young guy walked along the sidewalk that went past the back of the hotel.

"What are you guys doing?" he shouted. And he turned and started running to the front of the hotel.

I got really scared and started running too. I ran along the other side of the hotel, up to the main street and across to Mr. Rutherford's garage. Then I ran along the lane to our house. I sat on the swing in our yard, so that Mommy wouldn't ask me where I had been.

By supper time I heard adults talking about the guy who had seen us. They said he went running into the hotel and told everybody that there was a fire at the back of the hotel. All the men in the beer parlor ran to the back of the hotel and put the fire out. Denny's dad gave him a real bad spanking for stealing the matches and starting the fire.

Maybe Denny didn't tell on me. Mommy never got mad at me about the fire, but she did tell me that Denny had done it. Then she told me that just showed what a bad boy he was, and she told me again not to play with him. The next time I saw him I told him that my mom told me not to play with him. And then I ran away from him fast, so that he could not say that I had seen him set the fire. He didn't even chase after me then. So I didn't play with him any more.

But sometimes, when Denny was somewhere else, I would walk behind the hotel. Along the back wall, almost as high as the second floor, was a big black mark where the fire had burned the paint off the wall.

Reading and Writing in Two Language

One morning when we were visiting Yorkton for the summer I went downtown with Mommy to see a dentist. We didn't have dentists in Garrick, and we didn't have a dentist in Nipawin, like we had Dr. Fitton to see if we were really sick or like Mom had to go there when Polly was born. The dentist said there was nothing wrong with my teeth, but then he said that Mommy would have to wait another hour because of some long thing he explained to her. I asked her if I could go back home to Babba and Dedda's house by myself, and she said it would be okay. So I left her in the dentist's office and walked up the hill to to Second Avenue South by myself. When I walked into the kitchen Babba was sitting at the table, but instead of playing her game of solitaire, she was reading the newspaper. Babba and Dedda didn't get the paper every day, like my Daddy did at home, but every so often Dedda would go down to Broadway Avenue and buy a paper.

Babba looked up from the paper and said, "The paper says there was a big storm in Vancouver last night, Ruthie? I hope my sister is all right."

"Is that your sister who lives in Vancouver?" I had met this lady in the summer that she had come to visit Yorkton for a holiday. I remembered her because she looked much like Babba, but she was shorter, and she looked almost exactly like my mother.

"Yes," said my Babba. "That's her. We were such good friends when we were girls on the farm. She married Nick, and he got a job in Vancouver. It was a good job. That's why they have that big house she lives in, the one where you can see the water from her window." I remembered seeing a picture Babba had of a house that seemed to be sitting on a cliff high above a river. And a big bridge in the background. Babba told me that the tall buildings were in the city of Vancouver.

"But Dedda has a good job too. We don't have any big cliffs over the river or the ocean here in Yorkton. But this house is just as good as Auntie Anuta's." For a moment I was sorry for saying anything, and I kind of expected her to start complaining about my Dedda, as she often did. But she didn't answer, so instead I changed the subject.

"You stay in touch with your sister, don't you?"

"Oh, yes, Ruthie, we do. Sometimes we phone, but mostly we write letters."

That interested me, mainly because I knew from other stories, on other afternoons, that my Babba's education was a long story. Or maybe a short one. She had never been to school. After landing in Canada, the people from her village in Russia had moved out to Saskatchewan where they farmed. The religious views of the Doukhobours did not approve of education in schools. I thought from what I heard that they believed this education thing got in between the individual person and God. Singing was good, but not reading and writing.

"Did Dedushka beat your sister too, when she tried to learn to read?" I asked this because I remembered Babba once telling me a story about something that happened when she was a girl on the farm. Her cousin, Stephan, could read. One day she was in the barn with him. They had a book, and he was teaching her how to read the words. Her father, my Dedushka, walked into the barn and found them with the book. She told me that he grabbed a stick and beat her. He told her never to try and read again. It was bad.

"But," I had said when she told me the story, "Stephan could read. Was that OK?"

"Ah," she answered me, "But I was a girl. A boy could do these new things in Canada. But a girl? To read? This was a bad thing to my father."

"But you can read," I said, "You can even read in Russian and in English." As I talked to her I remembered the days that I had come over to visit her and found her sitting at her table with a book that I still had a copy of at home. My brother and I had used it too, and I had seen a copy of it in the library at my school. This book had a section for every letter of the alphabet. It had coloured pictures and little drawings to show how to write and print every single letter of the alphabet in English. There had been many days when I had come to visit Babba, that I had found her, with some paper on the table, practicing writing the letters of the alphabet.

I was remembering that when I said to her, "So Auntie Anuta can also write. Did Dedushka beat her too?"

"No. I don't remember that," said Babba, "but after that first time, we were very careful when Stephan brought the book out. We made sure that we did not get caught again."

"And, well, Ruthie, there was lots of work to do on the farm. We did not have much time for things like reading."

"But you and your sister can write to each other now, whenever you want to? Do you write in English or Russian?"

"Yes. We write letters to each other a lot. Russian is hard. We talk in Russian, like I talk to Nena in Russian. But my sister and I write most words in English. I think you might not be able to read it. We don't use those modern things that you use when you write, like those periods and question marks."

Working in Canada

Dedda didn't come to Canada on the same ship that Babba and her family did. He told me that he was already grown up when he came. He said that he was related to the Verigan family. They were the leaders of the first group that came out to farm in Saskatchewan. For some reason the son of Peter Verigan went back to their town in Russia a few years later.

He talked Dedda into coming back to Canada with him. Dedda once told me that what he really missed from his village in Russia were the cherries.

"Oh, Ruthie," he said, "the cherries, when they ripened, they tasted so good. Nothing like them here in Canada."

He also remembered passing through the city of Berlin in Germany. "What a great city," he said to me. "The city that Bismark built." Well, I didn't know anything about this Bismark, but Dedda didn't talk much about crossing the ocean, like Babba did. He talked more about finding work and getting settled out in Saskatchewan.

He said he didn't like working for other people. He sounded really mad when he told me about one time when a man who was going to hire him grabbed his arm to feel how strong his muscles were.

"He grabbed my arm and felt my muscles, Ruthie. It was like they treated the black man in that book, "Uncle Tom's Cabanya." Well, I didn't know that book, but I knew that by the time we used to visit Yorkton, Dedda worked for himself, and built houses and sold them and rented them. I never saw him grab the muscles of one of the Russian men who worked for him.

The Catalogue

When I was little in Garrick, we always got Eaton's catalogue in the fall before Christmas and in the spring before school was out. I'm not sure how Mommy got it. I think it came in the mail. But I loved it.

When we got the fall catalogue, my brother, Peter, and I would start by looking for toys. What did we want to ask Santa for at Christmas? There were lots of dolls, and I liked trying to pick the one I wanted. Peter always looked at toy trains. Maybe Santa would bring him one, maybe one with a long railway track that went in different directions, not just in one circle. Maybe a passenger train, then maybe some freight cars to go with the engine.

I told him he should ask for a caboose too. They were a neat part of a train. Whenever we took the real train to visit Yorkton, I loved to go and stand on the back platform of the caboose and watch the tracks as they got to look smaller and smaller behind us. Mommy didn't want me to do this. She would come out onto the caboose railing and make me go back into the train seats.

"It's dangerous to stand there, Ruthie", she said.

"No, Mommy, it's fine. There's a railing. I won't jump over the railing."

She still said, "no". So I had to sneak out there.

But I didn't have to sneak the Eaton's catalogue. Mommy let Petey and I read it as much as we wanted. We looked at it all the time, sometimes we argued about which part to look at. One time we tore it by accident. But it was only a small corner of one page that got torn.

Lots of winter snow to play in. Kids in the picture are
Ronnie, Peter, Faye, Donny and Ruth.

Faye and Elaine, weren't allowed to look at their Eaton's catalogue whenever they wanted. Mrs. Rutherford kept it on a little shelf on the wall of their house. They had to ask her if they wanted to look at it, and if she let them, she made them sit at their table while they looked. If their brothers wanted to look too, they might argue about which pages to look at, and then their mother would take it away and put it back on the shelf. She told them that people had to be careful with a book and keep it neat and tidy.

Petey and I looked as much was we wanted. One year Mommy told me I should pick out a new winter parka for myself. They had all different colours in the catalogue. Red was always my favorite. Some had fur around the edges of the hoods. Once I picked out a red one that Mommy said cost too much money, so I went back to look again. I must have found one that cost less money because we ordered a red one with a collar of black fur and knitted cuffs inside the bottoms of the sleeves.

I liked the cuffs because I they would keep the snow out of my sleeves if we were rolling around in the snow or maybe making snowballs to throw at each other. Mommy ordered that one. I remember that it didn't take long to come from Eaton's along with all the letters and packages that came on the train.

One of the things I wanted for a long time was a cowgirl outfit. We didn't have a movie theater in Garrick, but sometimes the adults in town would arrange to show a movie in the Legion Hall. I liked the western movies with the cowboys and cowgirls the most. Some of them had the same cowboys and cowgirls that they had in the plays I listened to on the radio. It took me a long time to get Mommy to order me a cowgirl outfit, but then she agreed. It had a bright red long-sleeved blouse with a sleeveless vest over the top of the blouse and a skirt with fringes on the belt and on the hem. I thought I looked like Dale Evans!

We ordered winter boots from the fall catalogue. Sometimes they didn't fit quite right, and Mommy would send them back to get a different size. When we got the Eaton's spring catalogue, we would order sandals for summer. One summer my sandal strap broke in, maybe, July. I wanted a new pair. Mommy said, "No". She said we couldn't afford it. I should have been more careful with the sandals. So I went barefoot for the rest of the summer. I didn't really mind. The dirt roads in town had soft black dirt.. that didn't hurt my feet. The two main roads were gravel. That was harder to walk on, but they had the wooden sidewalks next to them. We ordered the shoes for school in the fall. School shoes were the kind that covered your whole foot and had laces in the front. The catalogue had different shoe colours. It had socks, too, but sometimes we could get socks in Daddy's store in town. Sometimes in the fall, we went with someone who had a car, and drove into Nipawin to buy these things from the bigger stores.

But there was one thing I really didn't like about the catalogue. When the summer catalogue came, we really didn't need the winter catalogue any more. So Mommy and Daddy would put it in the toilet. Right beside the toilet seat, where the hole was.

Sometimes in the winter Mommy and Daddy let us use the metal toilet in our bedroom, but Dad had to empty the pail in that toilet every day or else it smelled up the house. So most of the time we were told to use the toilet outside. It was about half way along the short little path between our house and Daddy's store. It had one hole. Some people in town had two holes, but ours had a white plastic seat around the hole and a lid that closed. That was nicer to sit on than just plain wood.

The thing about using the old catalogues for toilet paper was that the catalogue pages were shiny and slippery. I hated that.

The real toilet paper, that came in rolls, was the best. The newspapers that also came on the train, and that Daddy read in the evening, were sometimes in the toilet, and they were a little bit soft. But the catalogue pages were shiny and awful. Sometimes you ended up with yucky poo on your fingers.

But then we would still have the new catalogue in the house, and it was always fun. School clothes, games, school scribblers, crayons and pencils, ski pants and things to ask Santa for were there in the fall catalogue. In the spring catalogue, there would maybe be a bathing suit for holidays or blue jeans or a summer T-shirt or maybe toys for friends' birthdays. Or new sandals. We always had fun looking at Eaton's catalogue.

Christmas in Strongfield

The first time I remember going to visit Grannie and Grampa Woodward was one Christmas. I think it was before my sister, Polly, was born, so there was just Petey and me with Mommy and Daddy. We took the bus from Garrick to Strongfield. I watched the snowy winter roads as the bus rolled along. Sometimes I could see trees along the side of the road, but for most of it, we were moving through snowy farm fields, with the flat prairie stretching off into the distance.

Grannie and Grampa still lived in the house where my Daddy had grown up. I remember that I liked the front porch. It had windows all around it, and you could look out and see some of the other houses in town and the church down the street. And lots of snow everywhere. But I had to put my parka on to go out and sit there, because it wasn't warm like the rest of the house.

Petey and I were sleeping in the room that Daddy said had been the bedroom for him and his brother Jack when they were boys growing up. It was one of the rooms at the top of the stairs that went up from the big room on the main floor, which the grown-ups called the living-dining room. There were two cots in the bedroom with a little space in between them and a window looking out onto the street and the wooden sidewalk. There were also other bedrooms upstairs. The one they said was Grannie and Grampa's, was the biggest, but I didn't go in there much.

We had our Christmas dinner at at big table in the living-dining room, and I remember that Grannie had Daddy and Grampa help her move the kitchen table into that room, so that there was enough room for all of us to sit down for Christmas dinner.

Dad told me that Grampa had built this house himself, way back when he and Grannie had first moved to Strongfield. Maybe it was too big for them once Daddy and his six brothers and sisters had grown up and moved away. I thought about this because all my later visits to Grannie and Grampa were in the summer holidays. On those visits they lived in a smaller house attached to the back of the post office. It only had two bedrooms. There was a small one next to the kitchen where we kids would stay when we visited in summer. If there were too many of us visiting, one of us slept on the chesterfield. Grannie and Grampa's bedroom was at the front of the house. It was just behind the post office, and it had a door that went into the back part of the post office, behind the counter where people came to get their mail. Grampa would go there every day to do his work.

He was the town postmaster. Every day, but not on Saturdays and Sundays, the train would bring the mail into town. Grampa had a big wagon that he pulled down the main street to the railway station. The mail for Strongfield would be dropped off from a train car, and he would pull the wagon back down the street to the post office. Then he took the mail into the back room. If there were parcels, he put them on a table. All the letters, he would sort and put them into rows of boxes on the wall. If you walked around to the front of the post office, you could see that the fronts of the rows of boxes had little doors on them with numbers on the doors. Each box belonged to one of the people in town. The post box number was part of their address if someone was sending them a letter. I knew that because Grannie and Grampa had their own mail box. When I wrote to them during the year, I first put their name down on the front of the envelope, then their mail box number, just before the name of the town and then the name of the province of Saskatchewan. Mommy had shown me how to address letters this way after I learned how to spell in school. When we got letters in Garrick, we had a mailbox in the Garrick post office too.

Somebody once told me that, before he ran the post office, Grampa had worked at a company in Strongfield that sold farm machinery. That must have been before I was born. There was no company selling farm machinery in town when I used to go and visit in the summer. But it made me think about asking Grampa if he had ever thought of farming when he first came to Canada.

By the Light of the Coal Oil Lamp

Then he told me a bit about himself. He told me he had been born in Yorkshire, England. As a boy he wanted to be a school teacher. In those days, he explained, you could start out as something he called a "pupil-teacher". That meant that he was in the classroom helping out the teacher. Then the teacher would sometimes tell him how to teach a class, and he would do the teaching, so that he could learn how to teach. I never did quite understand how that all turned out, but he said that he did teach school in a small Saskatchewan town when he first came to Canada. Most of the students were farm kids, and he thought they were much too rough and tough, so he thought he would quit teaching.

It was then, he said, that he thought maybe he should try farming. There was a system then, he said, where the Canadian government was giving people land. Some people said the land was free. Grampa said he had heard that it cost ten dollars, and what you would get was a quarter section of land. If you started farming it in your first three years, then it became your land. You owned the farm.

"I had the ten dollars," he told me. He went on to say that one morning, he and a friend decided to join a line outside a government office. The line was all men who wanted to get one of the quarter sections of land. The office was closed in the morning when he and his friend joined the line. Grampa's story went on, and he told me that they waited and waited, and the line got longer and longer behind them. They talked about how much time it was taking, but they thought maybe that was how these government offices worked.

Then he and his friend noticed that there was a little cafe across the street. "So", he told me, "we decided to go and have a cup of coffee while we waited for the land office to open." "Well," Grampa, continued, "by the time we got back, we saw that the line was gone. We went into the government office to ask what had happened. They told us that all the land had been given out."

"So, Ruthie," he ended his story, "that is why I did not become a Saskatchewan farmer."

After Grampa told me that story, I asked Grannie if she had wanted to farm when she first came to Canada. "Well," she told me, "I came because your Grampa was the only man I ever loved. Before we got married in England, he told me that he wanted to go and teach school in Canada.

When I grew up in Bath in England, my family was not rich, but we weren't really poor either. Sort of in the middle. If a young woman didn't get married the only thing things she could do was be a "lady's companion" to a rich older woman. I really did not like that idea one bit. So I agreed to go to Canada with Grampa. He said he would find a situation to settle in in Canada, and then send me the ticket to go and join him. He sailed from England, and we wrote letters until I got the letter sending me the ticket to go to Canada. It was a long trip across the ocean and across the country.

He met me at the train in Saskatchewan, and drove me with a horse and wagon to the small house he had started building. We went inside. I was hot and tired, and I said to him, "Reg, I would like to have a bath." Well, he went outside and came back with a pail of water. "I was so surprised, Ruthie. The water had pieces of stuff floating in it."

She always said that as if the "stuff" was really awful, but I never heard what happened next. Or before Grampa finished the house. Or before she lived in a town with a well that gave her clean water. And a stove to heat it on.

I did hear, though, that her second daughter, my Auntie Louise,was born in England. Grannie had gone back to visit family with her oldest daughter, Gwen, and came back to Canada with two little girls. She never returned to England. But she did talk her sister in Bath, who was also named "Gwen" to come to live in Saskatchewan. Auntie Gwen and Mr. Foster came to Canada and had two little girls of their own.

A Cold Frozen Death

It was February after supper, and it was dark outside. I was sitting next to the radio, waiting for the mystery program that I always listened to on Sunday nights. It was early. Some news came on, so I listened to that.

It sounded really bad. It was talking about a traveling salesman. OK, I knew what a traveling salesman was. Sometimes they came through Garrick. They had things in their cars to sell. I was in Daddy's store once when one of them came in. He had packages of things that men might buy to wear. I remembered socks and winter gloves and shirts. He wanted Daddy to take some of them to sell in his store. They talked for a while and then the salesman went out to his car and got some more packages of things for men to wear. I don't think Daddy bought any. I didn't see any in the store later. Then the man asked Daddy about Mr. Mitchell. He owned another store down the street.

Mommy and Daddy weren't close friends with Mr. Mitchell. They were both trying to get the people in town to buy from their store, and not the other person's store. But Daddy said nice things about Mr. Mitchell to the salesman. Then the salesman took his packages and went down the street to Mitchell's store. I don't know if Mr. Mitchell bought anything.

Another time a traveling salesman came to Daddy's store with magazines. They had pictures in them of furniture and pillows and tablecloths. They looked a little like Eaton's catalogue, but with not so many pages. Daddy took some of the magazines, and said to the salesman that he would give them to some other people he knew in town. After the man left, he laughed as he gave one to me, and said, "Here, Ruthie. It's like the Christmas catalogue. You and Petey can cut out the pictures or colour them." I took them, and Petey and I did have fun cutting them out and making pretend houses.

So I knew what a traveling salesman was. But the radio program said that one of them had frozen to death. That sounded really bad. It was like something I'd read in a story, maybe a fairy tale, the scarey kind that had witches and goblins in it.

Daddy was sitting on the chesterfield reading his paper, so I asked him if he had heard what they had just said on the radio. He put down his paper, and said,

"Yes. That's pretty tragic."

"How could he get so cold he could die?", I asked.

"Well", said Daddy, "It's happened before. It's these cold winters out here on the prairies. Those salesmen travel around a lot in their cars. The radio said this one ran out of gas."

"But couldn't he go somewhere like Mr. Rutherford's garage and get more gas?" I asked again.

"Well," said Daddy, "the announcer said that he was on a road between two towns when he ran out. I've heard that some traveling salesmen carry an extra can of gas in the trunks of their cars just in case they run out of gas alone on a road. But they said earlier that this man didn't do that."

"Why not?" I asked.

"I don't know," answered Daddy. "You heard the radio just now. The news announcer said that his family wondered why he didn't do that. But he didn't. It sounds as if he left his car and tried to walk to the next town for gas. Or maybe he hoped he could find a farm house and go in and get warm. And maybe get some help."

"Did he just lie down on the road?" I asked.

"Nobody knows, Ruthie," Daddy said. "They only found him two days later. His body was lying dead on the side of the road. He was quite far from his car. And far from any farm houses.

"He was all alone. It's so sad." I said.

"It is that indeed." said Daddy. He went back to reading his paper.

My radio program soon came on, and I forgot about the traveling salesman dead in the snow, alone beside the road.

But it wasn't the last time that winter that we heard on the radio about a traveling salesman who froze to death when he ran out of gas on a lonely freezing Saskatchewan winter road.

Climbing the Windmill

There were lots of windmills around when I was little. The town of Strongfield, where Grannie and Grampa lived, had one for the town well. But it was bigger than the windmills on peoples' farms. The bottom of it wasn't just standing on the ground. It was inside a wooden house, something like a toilet in somebody's back yard. Only it was a lot bigger than a toilet. And you didn't go in to go poop, you went in with a pail so you could pump it full of water.

One thing that was something like the outhouse was the bench. But where the hole would be in the outdoor toilet, instead there was a pump in the middle of the bench, and then people could put their water pails on the rest of the bench. If they had two pails, they could put the full one on the bench and then pump the second one full of water.

Two pails of water was as much as most people could pump because they only had two hands to take their pails of water home. But they could get more water if they had more pails. Then they could take another person, or one of their kids, and get four pails of water at once.

But I thought the little house at the bottom of the Strongfield windmill was scarey. Even on a hot summer day, when I walked in I suddenly felt the damp air on my skin. I heard the water dripping down the sides of the walls. I felt damp puddles on the floor under my bare feet. It was darker than outside. I thought I was in a cave, like in some of the fairy tales I had read.

"It's damp inside because it has no windows, Ruthie," was what Grannie told me. "But there's nothing scarey there. The windmills at the top turn so they can run the pump. Otherwise we would have no water in town. You must be brave when I send you for a pail of water," she said.

But I was always afraid of going into the damp misty room. I filled Grannie's pail of water as fast as I could pump, so I could get out of there.

There were some windmills that I really liked though. Those were the ones on peoples' farms. The bottoms of those windmills just stood on the ground outside, not in a scarey place. The parts on the ground were like triangles made out of steel pieces going up one on top of the other. Then they had a ladder in the middle. My favorite part was where the ladder went right up to the windmill blades at the top. I could watch the blades circle round and round in the wind. Those windmills on farms were taller than peoples' houses, even two-storey houses.

I remember another windmill from one day when our family went to visit another family, who were friends with Grannie and Grampa, on a farm.

I didn't know the other kids there, but the adults told us to go out and play. When we went into the yard at the back of the house, I saw that they had a windmill standing there. The other kids ran toward the barn, but I went over to look at the windmill.

The steel steps on the ladder came right to the ground, and then I was standing right in front of it.

I stepped on the first step of the ladder. It was made for a tall, grown-up person, but I got my first foot on to it, and then I pulled my second foot up beside it. The second step seemed a little high too, but I made it. Then I made the third step of the ladder.

I looked up at the blue sky and the sunshine. It was beautiful, and further above me, I could see the windmill blades turning in circles. I kept climbing.

Suddenly I heard a shout. "Ruthie, get down!" It sounded like Mommy, so I held my hands tightly on the side of the ladder and looked down.

It was Mommy shouting at me. Daddy was there too, and there were the four other adults who had all been visiting in the house. They all started yelling at me.

"Get down right away." "The blades will cut your arms." "The windmill will kill you." "You'll fall, Ruthie."

It sounded bad. So I hung tightly on to the sides of the ladder, and I looked up.

"It's okay," I called down to all the adults, who were still yelling.

"The blades of the windmill come farther out," I said, "I can go between them and the ladder.

"No, no," I heard Mommy shout. "You can't do that. It's not safe."

Then I heard Daddy's voice. "Ruth, come back down this very minute. If you don"t, I will have to spank you."

"Oh." I stopped on the ladder. Daddy never said he would spank me or Peter, unless we were doing something really, really bad.

I still thought I would fit between the ladder and the blades. I wanted to be part of that whirling in the sunshine. But I didn't want a spanking. I remembered once when Daddy had spanked me. It hurt. And it made me think I was stupid.

So I started climbing down. I heard all the adults cheering and saying things like "good girl" and "yay Ruthie".

I was still on the bottom step when Mommy grabbed me and hugged me.

"Oh, thank God," she was saying. The other adults were saying things like "That was a close one." "Maybe she would have fit." "How can kids be so stupid?" "Mr. Branski should put a fence around the windmill." "There's lots of other windmills".

Daddy put his arms around me and Mommy together. I didn't get a spanking.

But when we were back home and I told Faye and Elaine about what happened, I said that there really, really was enough room for me between the ladder and the windmill blades.

Tans in the Sunshine

When we kids spent a lot of time in summer playing outside, some of us would get something the adults called "sunburn". Our skin would get red, and sometimes it would hurt for a few days, but not for very long. Some kids' moms would make them wear a long- sleeved shirt if they went outside. They said the sunburn was caused by the sun shining on their bare skin. Sometimes kids got it on their noses and their cheeks too.

I didn't get this sunburn very much. When I played outside, my arms and legs and my face too, didn't get red. After a few days of playing outside with no long sleeves, my skin wouldn't get red. It would get a sort of brown colour. By the end of summer, I was very brown.

I liked this. It didn't hurt, like the kids who got sunburn said their skin hurt. It looked nicer to me than the pale white skin I had under my clothes in the winter.

Faye had blonde hair, and she got a lot of sunburn in spring. She said Mrs. Rutherford had told her it was because she was blonde, and that maybe she should go outside with long sleeves sometimes. But Faye said she didn't care, because beautiful movie stars were blonde, and she was like them. I said we didn't know any beautiful movie stars, so that didn't matter. Anyway I liked my brown hair, especially because my eyes were brown too. My brother, Peter, had blue eyes. He also got sunburned more than I did. But not as much as Faye.

Daddy had brown eyes too. He was a grown-up, so he didn't play outside and he wore a shirt when he was in the store. But he told me that he used to get the same brown tan that I did when he was a little boy playing outside.

Sometimes, he remembered, times when he had gone to a beach or a lake with his family. He said that then his skin would tan like mine did.

"We inherited this, Ruthie." he explained to me. "You know that your Grannie Woodward came from England."

"I know that, Daddy. Grannie Woodward likes to talk about growing up in the town of Bath."

"Yes," said Daddy, "And Bath is not far from the English Channel."

"And", he continued, "a long time go, in 1588, the King of Spain tried to invade England. He sent a big number of ships to the English Channel, filled with soldiers who were going to land and defeat England in a war. Well, Queen Elizabeth the First and Sir Francis Drake defeated the Spanish ships. They totally won the war. Many of the ships were destroyed and sank. But all the Spanish soldiers and sailors on the ships weren't killed. A lot of them drowned, but not all of them. Some of them swam to shore. They mixed up with the English people. But Spanish people had a little bit darker skin, and more of them had brown eyes. Then some of the English people might have had children with darker skin. It was the same thing with brown eyes. When I was a boy, your Grannie told me that not too many English people had brown eyes before the Spanish sailors landed on the shores of the English Channel.

"Your Grannie said that her Dad, whose name was Mr. Reiman, told her that his parents had told him that story. There had been many years of brown eyes in England since those Spanish soldiers and sailors were washed ashore."

"And now," said Daddy, "you and I are here in northern Saskatchewan with brown eyes. And we don't get a bad sunburn when the summers get hot. And it's all because of the Spanish Armada a long, long time ago."

When I told this story to my friend, Maureen, she said, "That's stupid."

When Maureen said that, Mrs. Larsen was standing in the store. Maybe she was there to bring Daddy our Sunday chicken, but she looked down at Maureen, and said,

"No. it's not stupid at all. Different groups of people are different. My grandfather came from Sweden to a part of the United States called Minnesota. He started farming there. Then when I was little my father came up to southern Saskatchewan and farmed there. That's where I met

Mr. Larson, and he was also from Sweden. All the Swedish people I know have blonde hair. And, Maureen, you look right now and see that I am wearing a long-sleeved shirt. On a hot sunny day like today, I will get a sunburn if I wear short sleeves. Mr. Larson wears long sleeves when he is out plowing on his tractor. And look at Ruth's Daddy here. He is wearing a shirt with short sleeves today. So you are wrong, Maureen. Stop making fun of Ruthie."

"I'm not wrong," said Maureen, and she ran out of the store.

"Silly child," said Mrs. Larson to Daddy.

"You're right," Daddy said to Mrs. Larson. "We're all different in some ways. But we can all try to get along. And can I get you something here in the store this morning?"

Mr. Ackerman's Store

Mr. Ackerman had the biggest store in town. You walked up the dirt road, past the Schindel's house, then past the Anderson's house, and then across the train tracks.

The store was on the other side of the ditch that ran along the train tracks. Where the road crossed the train tracks, the tracks were higher than the road. It was as if the road ran up a little hill and down the other side.

The door into the store was on the road, then the rest of the store went back in the same direction as the train tracks. Everybody in town said that Mr. Ackerman lived at the back of the store.

I didn't go to the back of the store very much. But I did it one time because I wanted to see if it was true that he had a house at the back. Well, there was no house, but there was a door, an ordinary door with a door knob. I was surprised when I saw a big sign on the door. It said KEEP OUT! In big red capital letters.

I looked around and saw that Mr. Ackerman was away at the front of the store. I thought about trying to see if the door would open. Maybe he had a kitchen there? Or other rooms? Then I got scared he might catch me. I didn't like getting in trouble.

So I started walking back to the front of the store. I went through the shelves full of bags with names on them like "fertilizer". I was good in school. I had learned how to sound out letters, so I could figure out a word. Sometimes I didn't know what the word meant. But when I sounded out that word, I knew that fertilizer was something people put in the dirt around their plants or in their gardens. Mommy told me that it made things grow better. She told me farmers sometimes used it, but they had so much land that it was hard to do. And very expensive.

There were also bags with other names on them. I didn't know what some of them were. After the bags, there were rakes and hoes hanging on the walls, and machines sitting on the floor. Some of those machines had wheels for driving. And some of them had parts on the front that looked like great big knives. I think those were for farmers.

I was getting into the part of the store where the kitchen stuff was, like plates and knives and forks and spoons. Then suddenly I saw that Mr. Ackermann was beside me.

"Are you thinking of buying something, Ruth?" he asked me.

I didn't want to tell him that I had gone to the back of the store to see if he really lived there. So I just said, "No."

"Well then," he said, "Maybe we can just get you back to the road so you can go home."

I followed him back to the front of the store. I was near the door going outside, and he went behind his counter where the money till was.

"Just a minute," he said. Then he reached under his counter. He came up and handed me a candy wrapped in paper. "Make sure you close the door behind you," he said, as I left, "and put the candy wrapper in that garbage can beside the door."

I didn't know Mr. Ackermann very well. I was kind of surprised that he was nice to me. I didn't have to be scared.

I didn't know much about him, but sometimes I heard the adults talk about him. Someone said he was a Jew. "What's a Jew?" I asked Mom.

"It's a religion," said Mom. "You know we talked about the Sunday School in the Orange Hall on Sundays. Mostly the preachers who come there are called Protestants. There is more than one Protestant religion. There is the United Church. I think they are made up of the Presbyterians and some other groups. Sometimes those preachers are Anglicans. That's the same religion as Grannie and Grampa Woodward. Do you remember hearing Grannie and her sister, Auntie Gwen, talking about finding an Anglican preacher to come to the church in Strongfield to give a Sunday sermon. Lots of people from England are Anglicans, I think. Then there are Catholics. They have a big important leader in Rome, in Europe, called a Pope. I think there are lots of Catholics somewhere in the world, But the Thompsons are the only Catholic family in Garrick."

"What about Babba and Dedda being Doukhobours?" I asked. "Is that a religion too?"

"Yes," said Mom, "but they're a bit different. They were not a whole big church, just one group of people. They were Russians, and they lived in the Caucasus Mountains in the southern part of Russia. They didn't have a Bible, and they did most of their religious ceremonies by singing. But one thing they believed in was that they were pacifists. Do you know what that means. Ruthie?'

"You told me that before Mommy, I said, "It means people who don't believe in war. They won't join armies. Like Uncle Walter during the war that ended when we lived in Strasbourg."

"Oh, that's right," said Mommy. So in Russia in the 1880s, the czar was jailing the young Doukhobour men because they would not join the Russian army. There was a famous Russian writer named Tolstoy, who was also a pacifist. He arranged with some English people in Canada to bring many Doukhobours here. The Canadian government liked the idea because the Doukhobours were good farmers. Babba's family came on the first ship. She was eleven years old when they came to Canada. They landed in Halifax and then they traveled out to Saskatchewan. Many of them lived near Blaine Lake. Remember when we went to visit Deddoushka Maloff. Well, he's Babba's Dad, and he was one of the first Doukhobour farmers in Canada. And remember that we went to see the Prayer Home in Verigin. The Doukhobours built that. It is like their church."

I remembered that visit. I also remembered Dedushka making funny faces and taking some wool from the spinning wheel in his house and putting it on his face like a funny moustach as a joke when he talked to me.

"So", Mommy finished, "you know, Ruthie, that I am not very religious. But that is my heritage as a Canadian."

Two Different Boys

Denise Fong and I were friends in Garrick, even if she was in grade three when I was in grade two. Her family lived in a house not far from the gate that went out of the school yard on the other side from the road. She lived with her brother and her Mom and with Charlie Fong, who had the grocery in town.

But she told me that Charlie was her uncle, not her Dad. Her Dad was Charlie's brother, and Denise said that he had died a long time ago when she was little. She didn't even remember much about him. They had lived in a different town then, she said and after her Dad died, they moved to Garrick where Charlie Fong had his store. Then the neighbours helped Charlie build a bigger house and she and her brother and her Mom moved in with Charlie.

But Mrs. Fong wasn't Chinese, like Charlie was. She was English, Denise said. "But she's my real mother. So Lenny and I are half-Chinese and half-English."

One of the things that was English about Mrs. Fong was the way she talked. Grown-ups said she had an English accent. When she talked, she sounded like the way people talked on the radio if they were doing a program about the royal family, or if King George was doing his talk on the radio on Christmas morning. Grannie Woodward sounded a little bit like that, but not so much as Mrs. Fong did.

She didn't talk to me very much. I liked her, and I thought she looked like a very beautiful lady. I wished she would talk to me, but if I started to ask her something like how did she come to Canada from England, or when did Denise's father die, she would say something like, "Why don't you go out and play, Ruthie." She always spoke quietly, but I always was afraid not to do what she said.

I also liked Denise's big brother Lenny. He was in the middle school building, the one just behind our grade 1, 2 and 3 building up the dirt road north of town. He talked to me sometimes. One day, I was telling him about the kit for building a model airplane out of balsa wood. Mommy and Daddy had bought it in Nipawin to give to Peter for his birthday. Then Lenny started telling me about how he had made some model airplanes out of balsa wood too. He was not a mean older boy.

The other English lady in town was Mrs. Haig. Teddy was the only child in that family, and he was in the same grade as Lenny.

Mrs. Haig called supper-time 'dinner-time'. I wanted to tell her dinner-time was in the middle of the day but I didn't tell her because she was a grown up. She also called the meal we ate in the middle of the day 'lunch'. So I asked her a question. A question was polite, to a grown up.

"But Mrs. Haig, isn't lunch some food, like maybe a sandwich that some kids bring to school in a bag so they can sit at their desk and eat it at school if their farm is too far from the school for them to go home at dinner-time? You don't sit down at a table and chairs for a lunch."

"No, Ruth," she answered me. "That is no excuse for bad grammar."

I didn't think my grammar was bad. She was just telling me I was wrong. Then she shook her finger at me and said, "You go home and tell your mother that dinner is the correct name for the evening meal. It is not called supper. But maybe people like your mother, whose parents were uneducated immigrants, might think that way."

I turned around and ran out of her yard. I didn't want to go home and tell Mommy what Mrs. Haig said. I think 'uneducated' meant the same thing as stupid, only worse. I went and found Faye to play with so I didn't have to tell Mommy.

Teddy Haig wasn't like his mom. He didn't talk about dinner and supper. He seemed kind of shy sometimes. But other times he would tell people they were wrong, like when Delores Schindel said her mother used to have T.B and that to cure it she had gone to the "san" until she got better

Then Teddy told her, "You are incorrect, Delores. What your mother had is correctly called Tuberculosis, not T.B. And the place where she went to be cured is called a sanitorium, not a san."

"But she's my Mom," said Delores, "And my Daddy said she was in the san for T.B."

"Well," said Teddy, "then they were incorrect, too." Delores was not a crybaby, but she ran away when he said that.

Sometimes kids made fun of Lenny and Denise, and Charlie Fong too, because they were Chinese. They would call them names.

One day I asked Mom about that. "Isn't it bad to make fun of Chinese people, Mommy?"

"Well, Ruthie," she said, "Let's just think for a minute that you're a grown up lady. You want to get married, OK?"

"OK," I said and I wondered why she was talking about me being a grown up. "So. Would you rather marry Lenny Fong or Teddy Haig?" she asked.

I started laughing. "Lenny Fong for sure. Teddy Haig is a stupid, stupid boy."

"Well," said Mommy, "You just answered your own question. There's nothing wrong about a person being Chinese".

Milk from the Farm

Besides being the only Catholic family in town, the Thompsons had more of a farm than most of the town people. Well, the Schindels had a farm too. Delores's Dad used to plow with his tractor in the fields that ran across the ditch beside the road where we walked along to school. The Thompsons lived on the other side of town, along the road that ran from the hotel past the restaurant and Mr. Rutherford's garage and Mr. Drumheller's butcher shop and Charlie Fong's store, then even further along that side of town.

Sheila was the oldest in the family. Carol was a year behind me in school. Even though their farm was in town, one of the things they had was cows. Most of us kids knew that you got milk from cows. Miss Zeorb explained that in school once, but everybody knew that already. Because he had these cows was why Mr. Thompson delivered milk to people around town. Mom told me one day about that. "Milk is good for you kids," she said, "so I pay Leo (Leo was Mr. Thompson's name) to deliver milk to our house every day. Some people use that Carnation milk that comes in cans. But I know that Leo milks his cows every morning, so we get real fresh milk. That's better than something in cans."

When I got a little older, I found out from Carol that sometimes it was her older sister, Sheila, who got up early in the morning to milk the cows. Carol was hoping to soon be old enough for her Daddy to teach her how to do it.

"I'd be like a grown-up person then," said Carol. "But maybe he'll pick one of the boys instead of me." She was a little bit sad when she said this.

I didn't know how to milk cows. When Carol said this, I thought it sounded a bit scarey. What if they stuck out their hoofs and kicked you?

What if they pooped in your face? But I didn't want to say that to Carol. She might think I was a sissy.

One thing her Dad did let Carol do was help put the milk in bottles. When we got it, on the step of our house, in the mornings, it was in glass bottles, with lids on them. They were the same as the glass bottles that I saw with milk in them in the stores in Yorkton. When we visited Babba and Dedda, we went to the store to buy milk in the glass bottles.

Yorkton was a city, so nobody had cows in their yards any more. Babba said they used to get milk from their cows when she was a little girl on Dedduska Maloff's farm, and then in their own barn in Yorkton when Mommy and her brother and sisters were little.

"Fresh milk is best, Ruthie," she said. Mommy said the same thing.

In the summer time, Mr. Thompson had his horse pulling the wagon where he had the bottles of milk. In the winter, he had the horse pulling a big long sleigh with a box of bottles on it. Daddy said those long flat sleighs were called toboggans. "Toboggan" was a word I heard on the radio when they were talking about some important races in some big city somewhere.

When we finished drinking the milk, Mommy would rinse the bottles with some rainwater from the oil barrel beside the back porch and leave the bottles outside on the step. Then Mr. Thompson would take the old bottle when he left the new bottle. That's how we got milk to keep us healthy.

Fowl Supper Time

The Orange Hall was on one of the two big main streets, right near the corner where one of the town wells was, the one where Daddy got the water for our house. In the school year, high school, the grades from seven and up, was held in that hall during the week. On Sundays, one of the churches had Sunday School in the Orange Hall. Most the kids from town, except the Thompsons, went there.

The much bigger building was called the Legion Hall. It was along the road out of town, over the railroad tracks, almost across from Mr. Ackerman's store. The Orange Hall was painted white on the outside, but the Legion Hall had no paint. The boards looked kind of faded gray, like some of the old farmhouses we would see if we drove to somewhere or maybe see from the train on the way to Yorkton. But it had big steps going from the road up to the front door. Inside there was a very big space.

Every year the ladies in town did something called a "fowl supper", and that was always in the Legion Hall. Mommy always helped with that. There was a big long table in the middle of the room. Somebody told me that the men in town had moved all the tables and chairs into their places.

One year I went with Mommy to the Legion Hall. She had baked a big pan full of macaroni mixed in with vegetables, and breadcrumbs and cheese on top. She called it a "casserole". Once it was cool from the oven, she wrapped it in two dishtowels from our kitchen. Then she put it into Peter's red wagon.

"That way there's no chance I might drop it," she said.

When we got to the Legion Hall, we left the wagon outside near the walls, and we took the casserole up the stairs and into the hall.

The big table already had some pans full of food on it, but Mommy said, "Let's go into the kitchen first."

Off to one side when you first walked in, there was a door that was open, and, as soon as we walked in, I could see it was a kitchen. It had cupboards all along one wall and a stove on the other side. There was another long table in the middle of the room, and it was covered with pans full of food and piles of plates and glasses and spoons and forks and knives.

Almost everybody's Mom that I knew in town was there. They were talking a lot to each other and moving things around. Mrs. Joseph picked up a pile of glass plates from the table and started carrying them to the door into the big room.

"Don't forget the knives and forks," said Mrs. Sullivan.

"Those are still in the drawers," said Mrs. Rutherford.

"Do you think the Legion has enough forks and knives?" said someone else.

Mrs. Joseph just kept walking through the door with the plates, and I saw her put them in a pile on the long table in the big hall.

"Where should I put this casserole?" said Mommy.

"It's not a dessert, so it should go out on the first table," said one of the other ladies, as Mom put it down on the table beside us.

There were already some other casseroles and pans full of vegetables and baked potatoes, and a big bowl of salad on the table. Then I was surprised at what I saw sitting on top of the stove. There was a whole row of chickens on top of a big pan. They looked just like the chickens that Daddy bought from Mrs. Larsen, the ones we ate for our Sunday supper, the ones that weren't Henny Penny or Turkey Lurkey. They were all brown and cooked.

"That's why it's called a fowl supper," said Mommy.

"But doesn't that word mean something really bad?" I asked. "Like the detective called that nasty man who stole jewellery on the radio program?"

"No," said Mommy. "That word is a different word that sounds the same as fowl."

Then she spelled it slowly for me. "It is spelled f-o-u-l. It means bad, awful, rotten. The man on the radio program was a bad, awful man, a jewelery thief."

"Oh," I said, "and what about the chickens then?"

"That word is spelled f-o-w-l." She spelled it really slowly again. I could hear that there was one different letter.

"It means a sort of bird-like farm animal. Like a chicken, maybe the same word for a turkey too. Some people, if they can go hunting for a wild animal, they might eat ducks. That would also be a fowl."

"I get it," I answered. I always liked spelling words, so I spelled them both out loud.

"You got it, Ruthie." said Mommy. "These fowls we eat are not foul." She laughed. Then I got that she was joking, and I laughed too.

"So, you see," she said, "We call it a fowl supper because chickens are the main course. I never heard of a fowl supper that had meat." I was happy I knew that.

Then I helped Mommy and the other ladies with getting dishes and other things out of the shelves and putting the food on the big tables out in the main hall. Then we set up all the smaller tables with chairs around them.

Later Daddy came over with Petey. It was starting to get dark outside, and he had closed the store. Soon some of the other men who worked in their stores or other places, came too. And some of the families from the farms around town.

People helped themselves to food from the big tables and then went and sat at the smaller tables to eat. Some sat at benches along the walls. Everybody talked and sometimes met up with friends they hadn't seen for a while.

After they had finished eating, the Boychuck family got up from their table and went over to some suitcases they had left in the corner of the room. I knew who the family was, and I was excited because I knew they played music. There was a stage at the front of the Legion Hall, and, when they got their instruments out of the suitcases, they went up on to the stage and started playing.

Everybody laughed and cheered.

Mommy and some of the other ladies started taking the empty plates and other dishes and the spoons and forks and knives back into the kitchen. There was a big sink at the back of the kitchen and a big square barrel full of water beside it.

"Good thing we got the tank filled this afternoon," said Mrs. Schindel. "I guess we better start heating the water for dishes."

"Look on the stove," said Mrs. Scott. "I've already done that."

Some of the ladies said they would stay and start the dishes. Somebody pulled a pile of dish towels out of a drawer near the shelves on the wall.

"Can I go out and watch them dance, Mommy?" I asked.

"Yes, you can," said Mommy, "and tell Daddy that I'll be out soon." And then she said, "Oh, and be sure you watch Petey. See that he doesn't get in any trouble."

I didn't like looking after Petey, because he wouldn't do what I said if he didn't want to, but I said, "OK", and ran out into the big room to watch the adults dancing.

The Boychuck family played and people danced for a long time. Us kids sometimes sat and listened to the music. What was left on the food table was mostly from the dessert. I ate some cookies and some slices of apples and oranges. And one raisin tart before they were all gone.

Petey ran with some of the little boys, and they didn't do anything bad. I got him two cookies, but I saw him getting one for himself later.

It seemed like a long time, and fun, before Mommy and Daddy stopped dancing and came to get us to go home. Some of the men were outside the door and talking about locking up the building later that night. As we walked across the field and down the lane to our house, Mommy carried the empty casserole pan and Daddy let Petey sit in his wagon and pulled him home.

Now that I even knew how to spell it, I couldn't wait for another fowl supper to happen

The Vaccination Van

One spring time, before school was out, I had the measles. That was the name of a sickness. I felt hot, and my skin was all covered with red marks. Mommy and Daddy let me lie in their bed in the day because they said that might help me get better. Then my Petey got the measles too. So they put some blankets and a pillow on the chesterfield in the living room, so he could lie there.

Then Mommy told me that Faye and Elaine and Larry had the measles too, and so did some other kids in town. After a few days I started to feel less hot, and then I asked Mommy to let me get up. She said I could get up, but I couldn't go outside because I wasn't cured yet.

"When will I be all cured?" I said. "What does cured mean?"

"Cured means better. Like you were before you got sick," said Mommy. "Maybe next week," she said, "but measles is catching, and we don't want to spread it to other kids. And we don't want you to get sick again."

A little bit after she let me get up, I started feeling really tired, then Mommy let me go back into my bed and sleep. So I guess I really was still sick.

After a few more days, I thought maybe I was "cured" because Mommy let me go out and play. Some of my friends told me that some other kids were still sick at home in bed.

When I went back to school, some kids were still not there.

But after a while, nobody had measles any more. But the adults didn't stop talking about measles and other sicknesses that kids had. Mommy told me that when I was really small, in Fort Frances, I had a sickness called chickenpox.

"That's a funny name. Was I really hot then too?" I said. I didn't remember this chickenpox, but Mommy showed me some marks on my chest. She said they were left there on my skin from when I had chickenpox. I didn't remember this.

But the grown-ups kept talking about us kids getting sick. There was something they called "vaccination." I think it had something to do with doctors. And maybe with the government.

Then one day this great big van came to town. It parked on the lane that went from our house, past the Rutherford's house and down to the corner between Daddy's store and the post office. The adults went around town getting all us kids to line up behind the van. It was a nice sunny day, so it was okay to line up along the lane.

Then the people who came in the van opened the doors at the back of the van and pulled out a step that went down on to the ground. One man and one lady who had come in the van went up into the van and sat near machines that were in there.

Delores's second brother, Jimmy, was the first kid in line. The lady in the van told him to come up the steps. When he did, she asked him to sit down on a chair. Then she pulled up the sleeve of his shirt and wiped his arm with some cotton batten that she had in a jar. Then I saw her pull a funny-looking thing, sort of like a pen with a pointed end out of another jar. She held it near his arm and squeezed it. Jimmy shouted out, "Ouch".

Then the lady said, "It's OK, we're finished. You can climb down now."

Then she asked Ronnie Emde, who was the next kid in line, to come up the steps.

"Will it hurt?" he said.

"Just a tiny little bit," the lady said. "I'm a nurse. Your parents have asked me to come to this town and vaccinate you kids. That way you won't get the measles. Or some other very bad sickness."

"Well, OK," said Ronnie. But I think he wasn't too happy. He said "ouch" too. Then, when he came down, Wayne was standing behind him. "It doesn't hurt much," he said to his brother.

Wayne went up next, and for a while all we kids in the line went up the steps and got the needle, then came back down again. Then anther person from the van looked at our arms and told us we were finished and that we could go.

Most of us didn't go anywhere when we were finished. It was fun watching other kids go up and down the stairs. Even the Scotts and the Larsons and the Jellisons, all the kids from the farms near town, were in the line. Lots of the adults were standing around watching too.

After a long time the line was finished, and every kid had been vaccinated. When I had my turn, it didn't hurt very much.

Then the people in the van packed up their boxes and things. They shut the big back door and climbed into their van, then drove up the lane, along the main street, over to the road past Mr. Ackerman's store, across the railroad tracks and out of town.

Later that night, when Daddy was reading the paper, I asked him what this "vaccination" was.

"Well," he said, "that needle you kids got to vaccinate you will prevent you from getting some serious diseases. You already had mumps and measles and chickenpox. But there 's whooping cough and diphtheria and tetanus too. One of my sisters died of diphtheria when I was just a boy in Strongfield. Peter never had chickenpox, so maybe he will not get it now."

"That's good, isn't it?" I said.

"Yes, it is," said Daddy. "People who live in bigger towns or cities can go to a doctor and get vaccinated. But you know that there are no doctors in Garrick. So some of us got together and wrote a letter to the government. They can arrange to send out the van and the nurses you saw today. So we got them to send it here to Garrick. We knew they were coming today. That's why all the kids from the farms were here too. It's good to prevent sickness. "

"Oh, I didn't know that," I said.

"Well, we love all you little kids. We wouldn't want you to get sick and die." Daddy said with a laugh. Then he went back to reading his paper.

The Big Sister

One night in Yorkton, before it got dark, I was riding bikes with Auntie Lydia. When we were on the road near the Yorkton Cemetary, she said, "Do you want to go and see your sister's grave, Ruthie?"

I didn't know what to say. Sister? Polly was my new baby sister, but she was at home with Mommy.

So I said, "What sister?"

"Oh!" said Auntie Lydia. "Didn't your mommy tell you about her? Your sister Neura? The one who died when she was a baby?"

"I don't know about that," I said. "What happened to her?"

"Well," said Auntie Lydia. "Maybe we should ask your Mom about this first. Should we go home and do that?"

"OK," I said. I really wanted to know what she was talking about. What was Mommy going to tell me. Somebody dead sounded scarey.

Mommy was home talking to Babba. I didn't see Peter around, and Mommy said Polly was sleeping.

Lydia said to Mommy, "I have to ask you something, Neen." So they went into the dining room, and I sat by the table with Babba. When Mommy and Auntie Lydia came back into the kitchen, Mommy said to me, "Ruthie, Lydia said she was going to show you a grave, but she suddenly realized that you didn't know you ever had another sister."

"That's right," I said.

"I'm so sorry, Ruthie," said Mommy, "but I didn't think you were old enough to learn about this. But now I will tell you."

She came and sat beside me and gave me a hug. Then she started talking. "Before you were born," she said, "Daddy and I had another little girl. We called her Neura. You know that's how we say my Russian name in English. She was a healthy little baby until she was three months old. Then she got sick and started coughing and spitting up. We took her to our doctor here in Yorkton. That's when Daddy and I were living here on Myrtle Avenue. The doctor said she had a lung infection. We tried to keep her warm and look after her. The doctor even sent to Winnipeg for a drug called penicillin that they didn't have here in Yorkton. It cost fifty dollars. That was more than Daddy and I had saved at the time. Babba and Dedda helped us pay for the drug. But it didn't help. Poor little Neura died. So you will never have a big sister."

I could see that Mommy had tears in her eyes. What should I say? A sister? I didn't know this.

Auntie Lydia was standing beside the kitchen table. "So you see, Ruthie," she said, "it was your sister Neura's grave that I was talking about going to see in the cemetery. I'm sorry I didn't ask your Mom about it before I told you."

"It's OK, Lydia," said Mommy. "Maybe I should have told her before. She's old enough to know. But I was just so sad." And Mommy's eyes filled with tears again. I was still scared to say anything. But then I thought about something.

"Auntie Lydia said there was a grave in the cemetery. Is this little baby buried there?"

"Yes," said Mommy. "We didn't want to forget her."

"Can I go and see her?" I asked.

"Well," said Auntie Lydia, "You can't see her, but I was going to show you her grave. Is that okay with you, Neen?"

"Yes," said Mommy, " I'd like to have her see it now that she knows about Neura." Then they both turned to Babba, and the three of them started talking in Russian. After a few minutes, Mommy turned to me and said, "Babba says it's too far for her to walk, but what if you and I and Lydia walk over to the cemetery, so we can show you Neura's grave."

"Yes, please," I said. I didn't really know what to say, but I really wanted to see the grave.

So Mommy and I and Auntie Lydia left the house and walked to the cemetery.

114

It wasn't that far. We walked through the gate and past a lot of other graves. Then we got to a little square stone flat on the ground. It said Ruth Neura Maude Woodward. Then it had two dates, April 6, 1940 - June 21, 1940. Mommy and Auntie Lydia stood there while I read it.

Then I said, "She's called "Ruth", like I am."

"Well," said Mommy, "We called her Neura. That's my name in Russian. You know that. "Maude" is part of Grannie Woodward's name. We still liked the name Ruth, when you were born, but we didn't want the exact same name."

"This is my big sister lying here under the ground," I said.

Mommy and Auntie Lydia both said, "Yes" at the same time. Then they both asked me if I wanted to stay longer and look at the grave. I said that I would because it seemed so sad, but it was strange too. I had a big sister, but not really. So I asked if we could walk home then, and if they would mind if I came another time. Mommy said that would be okay. And then she said too, "If you want to ask me anything more about Neura, you just ask. Okay?"

I said okay to that, and we walked back home.

I did walk over to the grave one more time that summer, but we didn't talk much about Neura. When I got home to Garrick later in the summer, I told Daddy that I knew about my dead big sister now. He told me how sad he had been when she died. Then he told me that he was the one who had gone to the people who ran the cemetery to arrange for her name to be carved on the stone and for it to have its place in the cemetery. Then they had their own little family ceremony to bury the body. And Daddy told me that her body was buried in a little coffin that Dedda made.

"Well," said Daddy, "You know that Dedda is a carpenter. He got out his wood and his tools in the backyard behind the house on Myrtle Avenue and he cried and carpentered, and he carpentered and cried. And I stood there and cried with him." And Daddy nearly started to cry when he told me this story.

The Swings

I always loved swinging. It was so much fun to sail back and forth through the air. Most of us kids knew that you could make yourself go higher if you bent your knees and pulled your legs up and then down again.

If someone was really little, you could push them when they sat on the swing, but if they were really little they might fall. But the little kids would still ask us bigger kids to swing them. It was best to ask the grown-ups for the really little kids.

There was a swing in the big grass space between the railway tracks and the street that Daddy's store was on. It was between the tracks and the poles where people tied up their horses when they came into town. The swing was there even when we first moved to Garrick.

Maybe some grown-ups early in the town built it. We kids called it "the town swing". It had two big high poles, with the pole across the top and big thick ropes hanging from the poles. The ropes went through round holes in the sides of the seat. That way the seat could never fall off or get lost. You could always sit down on the seat, grab the ropes and start swinging.

Petey and Ruthie on the town swings. The town elevators are along the railway tracks in the background.

Oh, but you couldn't always do that. On a sunny summer day, especially if there was no school, there might be other kids there. Then we had to take turns. Sometimes kids were mean and pushed to the front of the line.

On those days, I liked to go back down the lane to our house. We had two swings in our yard beside the house. Daddy built them soon after we moved there. We couldn't swing on the days Mommy did her washing because there were two clotheslines between the pole on both sides of the swings. Mommy didn't want us swinging in case out feet accidentally hit the wet clothes at the ends of the lines near the swings. But Mommy only did the washing every Monday. All other days we could swing.

The poles Daddy put up were not as high as the swing on the main street. But we could still swing back and forth between the poles at both ends of the clotheslines.

The wooden seats on the swings Daddy made were different too. The boards were good to sit on, but the sides did not have round holes, just a place where Daddy had cut a little space out of the sides of the board. The rope went around the bottom of the seat board. The seats on the swings were good to sit on because Daddy smoothed them with sandpaper. I helped him do that because I came out to the back porch when he was doing it, and he let me help him. He showed me how to hold the sandpaper so I didn't hurt my fingers.

The next night he had a can of paint and a brush. The paint was from his store. It was white, and Daddy said it was called "enamel", so it would be smooth to sit on. I asked if I could paint the seats. He let me do that, and then let me paint the second coat the next night. I got to stay up late two nights in a row. And I could see the seats that I made when I went on the swings in our yard. Sometimes, if Faye and Elaine, or one of my other friends, came over, I told them they could swing on my very own seats. They laughed, but I told them I really did do the painting.

But I always loved swinging. On anybody's swings.

Riding My Bike

When I was six, I got a bike early in the summertime. It came on the train in a box. It was a big long box, but sort of flat. Daddy got the box from the station. He carried it home and put it in our back porch.

He told me it was my new bike, but he said he would have to help me put it together. I would have to wait until Sunday, when he was not working in the store.

I was really excited, so I didn't really want to wait. And on Sundays Mommy and Daddy slept in. They didn't get up early in the morning, like on the other days of the week. Sometimes they let us get into bed with them. But I mostly liked doing that in the winter, when it was cold in the house, and Mummy and Daddy's bed was warmer than my top bunk.

Petey came with me on Sunday morning, but before we got into bed, I said, "Can we get up and open the box with my new bike?"

Mommy rolled over and put her head on one arm.

"No, Ruthie," she said. "You know we don't get up early on Sundays. Then we have bacon and eggs, our special Sunday breakfast. So you will have to wait a little while. But it looks like it's going to be a nice sunny day, so you'll have all afternoon to ride your new bike."

Well, I wished Mommy hadn't said that. Just then Petey said, "Can I ride it too?" I turned around and said, "No. It's my new bike. You're too little for a bike. You still have the tricycle."

"I'm not too little," said Petey. "I'm nearly four years old."

"Both of you be quiet," said Mommy. "Jump up into bed here with me and Daddy. We will do your bike later, Ruthie."

So Petey and I got into bed and cuddled up with Mommy and Daddy. Then we had our Sunday breakfast. Then Mommy put some water on the stove to heat up for doing the dishes.

"Oh," I thought, "Now I'm going to have to dry the dishes before I can open my new bike."

But then Daddy said, "Why don't we go outside and get your new bike ready?"

I was so excited that I ran out into the porch. Daddy followed me and carried the big box out the porch door and put it down on the flat stones outside. He had his tool box out too, and he pulled out a big knife and then started cutting the sides of the big box open. I could see that it was a red bike. My favourite colour! Then I could see the bike wheels.

Daddy pulled out some other parts and started putting them together. Soon a real bike was standing there on the stones.

"But before you can ride it," he said, "we have to blow up the tires. Mr. Rutherford has a hose for blowing up tires in his garage."

"Let's go there now," I shouted as I jumped up and down.

So Daddy lifted up the bike off the ground, and we walked across the lane, over Mr. Drumheller's yard and down the street to Mr. Rutherford's garage. He was there working on a machine, and Daddy asked him if we could use the hose to blow up the bike tires.

"Sure, Bert, go ahead," said Mr. Rutherford. "Nice new bike, Ruth," he said to me.

"Thank you, Mr. Rutherford," I said.

Mommy and Daddy had told me I should always be polite and say things like "please" and "thank you" to grown-ups. Anyway, Mr. Rutherford was a big man, and sometimes he was grouchy or he yelled at Faye and Elaine or their brothers. I was too scared of him to say anything except polite words.

Then Daddy blew up the tires. When he was doing it, he showed me how to work the hose. And he said, "You always have to be sure they don't get flat. So if you think they don't look right, come and show them to me. Okay?"

"Okay, Daddy," I said. "Can I ride it now?"

"Do you know how?" said Daddy.

"Yes," I said, "Sheila showed me how to ride on her bike before," I told him, and so he let me take the handlebars and jump my feet up ready to ride the bike.

I drove it out of Mr. Rutherford's garage onto the road. I didn't fall. I kept pedaling, and my bike moved up the street to the road that turned past Mr. Converoy's house and over to our lane.

When I turned down the lane, Daddy was just back from Mr. Rutherford's garage.

I stopped my bike and put my feet down on the ground. I was sort of afraid, but I didn't fall. Now I knew how to get on and off my bike. I walked it over to Daddy.

"This is good," he said. "You know how to ride already. You know how to pump up the tires. Everything is good, Ruthie."

But then he said, "Don't forget to put it in the back porch when you're not riding it. You don't want somebody to steal it."

"Okay," I said. Then I looked at my new bike again and said to Daddy, "The name on this bike is a SUN bike. Faye and Elaine's bike says it's a CCM. Mary Scott's bike says CCM too."

"They're all different bikes," said Daddy. "SUN is the name of an English bike." Then he laughed and said, "You're half English, Ruthie. Don't you want an English bike?"

I was not sure what to say. I thought it was a really nice bike. Then Daddy said, "No, that's not why I got it. I heard about it on the radio, and I went over to the post office and phoned the bike store. I got a very good price. And they are well made."

"I like it because it's red," I said. "Can I go riding some more?"

By then Mommy and Petey had come outside. "What a nice bike," said Mommy.

"Can I ride it?" said Petey again. This time Mommy said, "Maybe Petey. You can try it later. Ruthie just got her new bike, so we'll let her try it out today."

"Okay," said Petey, and he went back inside the house.

I got back on my bike and rode down the lane to Daddy's store, then along the front street toward the Schindel's house. At Mr. Lewis's garage, I turned and went up the road that went to school. At the little old house at the corner of our road, I turned back to our place.

Mommy and Daddy were back inside. I got off the bike and went in and told them where I had been on my ride. "It sounds as if you have gotten this bike-riding down pretty well," said Daddy. "You can go out again if you want to."

"Okay." I almost shouted because I was so excited. I rode around the streets of town for most of the afternoon.

As the summer went on, Mommy and Daddy would let me ride further. I went out on the road to school, then around the schoolyard and back down the road into town. Later I would take the same road in the opposite direction and go over the railroad tracks and down as far as the Scott's farm. Some days I would go up the lane and turn around to go past the hotel and out to the Emde's house. Ronnie said he was going to ask his Mom and Dad if he could get a bike too.

I loved riding my bike everywhere I could whenever there was sunny warm weather.

The Man in the Ditch

I never talked to this man, or met him. His name was Mr. Moore, and when some of the adults were talking about him, they called him Stan. I think he had a farm with his brother out on the road north of town, further than Mrs. Rutherford's brother's family, and he came into town one day late in the fall.

But I heard about it because for a few days all the adults in town were talking an awful lot about him. If we kids asked a question about what happened, the adults would say something like, "This is not something you children should hear about" or maybe they would say "This is a serious adult matter." But it was still easy to hear them talk to each other.

They said a friend had given Mr. Moore a ride into town, so he could buy some food and maybe other things. Other people said he only wanted to come into town to go to the beer parlour. Anyway, I guess he did go to the beer parlour in the Smith's hotel. Different men said they'd seen him there. Some said they talked to him. Some said he was pretty sober, some said he was pretty drunk.

I heard Daddy talking to Yvonne in the store. She said it was so so sad about what happened to Mr. Moore. Daddy said he agreed it was sad, pretty awful. But then he said that maybe Mr. Moore did have too much to drink. Maybe he should have stayed in the hotel overnight and gone back home in the morning.

The reason everybody was talking about Mr. Moore was because the next morning, somebody had found him face down in the water in the ditch beside the road. It sounded as if a bunch of men then came out from town to try to help. I heard them say that when they tried to revive him, they couldn't get him to breathe again. Mr. Moore was dead.

Someone else had gone to the town phone in the post office and called some government people or a hospital or somewhere. The adults were saying that an official person would soon come to take the body away and find out how he died. Someone else had driven up the road and brought his brother into town. The adults said there was no other family.

A lot of the talk was about Mr. Moore being drunk. Some people were saying how stupid he was, some people felt sorry for him. But nobody remembered seeing him walk out of town. And nobody knew how he got to be lying face down in the water in the ditch. And everybody said for sure that they didn't know how long it was before he died.

The official person came into town, and his brother went with them when they took Mr. Moore's body to Prince Albert. It was a while before his brother came back to Garrick. He said that a doctor told him it was true that Mr. Moore had died from drowning. Then he said that because he was the brother he had arranged for him to be buried.

By then most of the adults were not talking about him anymore.

The Big Sister
and the New Baby

Georgie Atkins was in my grade in school. His sister Jeannie was older than we were. She was in grade five when we were in grade two. They had a little brother younger than Georgie who wasn't in school yet. Their Dad had a farm up the road, over the railroad tracks and past Mr. Ackerman's store. But their house was in front of the farm fields, along the road, so Jeanie and Georgie could walk into town to play with the rest of us kids. Jeannie played with the older girls like Tina Lewis or Sheila Thompson.

But I liked playing with Georgie. Lots of times he would walk along the tracks with Faye and me. One summer he told us that his Mom was going to have a new baby. He was hoping it would be another boy in the family. "Jeannie's enough girls," he said.

"No," I answered, "if it's a girl, then you have two boys and two girls. That's more fair, because it's even."

"But," said Georgie, "you have you and your baby sister. Two girls isn't fair to Peter. So it's your family that's not fair."

Well, I didn't know what to say next, so I said, "I can beat you to the railroad tracks", and we both started running across the field.

We were closer to Christmas, and it had already snowed a lot when I heard the adults talking about Georgie's Mom going to the hospital in Nipawin to have the new baby. Jeannie and Georgie stayed home from school. I walked up to their house one day after school. When I went into the yard, Jeannie came running out.

"Go home, Ruthie," she said. "I'm looking after the house, and my dad told me not to let anybody in."

"Where's Georgie?" I said back.

"We've got chickens and pigs to feed. He's busy." she said.

I saw Georgie come up behind her, but she pushed him back into the house, then slammed the door shut.

I went home and asked Mommy why Georgie's parents were not home.

"Nobody's sure, Ruthie," Mommy said. "Georgie's mom had to go to the hospital in Nipiwin to have her baby.

"Like you did, when Polly was born," I said.

"Yes," said Mommy, "but it's been over a week and nobody has heard anything. But he's not a very friendly man. He doesn't know anybody in town well enough to phone from Nipawin to tell them how she is. Nobody knows them very well either."

"Well, Georgie's a nice boy," I said.

"Yes," said Mommy, "but everybody says Jeannie's dad told her to look after the house and farm and not to talk to anybody in town. Maybe he's trying to get a sister or aunt to come and help."

"Is there a new baby?" I asked.

"We don't know," said Mom.

Well, a few days later, we did know. Mommy said that the new baby was a boy. I thought to myself, "Well, Georgie will be happy."

But Mommy said too that she heard that Mrs. Atkins was dead. She died having the baby.

"Oh," I said, "that will make Georgie very sad. I should go and see him."

"Don't do that," said Mommy.."You know what happened the last time you went to their house. Remember Jeannie wouldn't let you in. And her dad and the baby aren't here yet. He must be looking for someone to look after the baby. You mind your own business for this, Ruthie."

"Okay, Mommy," I said. And I didn't go.

Later we heard that Mr. Atkins had come back from Nipawin with the baby. But it was winter, and Christmas was coming, we had school holidays, and so I didn't see Jeannie and Georgie for a while. When school started again after the hollidays, Georgie was back at school, but Jeannie wasn't. So I talked to Georgie at school and asked him what had happened.

"My new brother is named Frederick," he said, "and Jeannie is looking after him. We have a baby bottle and diapers and a new blanket for the crib. Jeannie said I should do the dishes after supper, but my Dad said that was women's work and my job is to help feed the pigs and the chickens and help him in the barn." He laughed and said, "I like that better than doing the dishes."

"What happened to your Mom?" I said.

"She's dead. Gone. You know that," he said. "Let's go and make some snowballs before recess is over." Then he ran across the school yard and I followed him.

Jeannette didn't come back to school. When spring and the warm weather came, I walked up to their house one Saturday. Their Dad was standing behind the gate when I got there. He said a swear word and told me to go back to town. I was scared, so I did.

A long time went by, and soon it was almost Christmas again. I heard Mrs. Mitchell talking to a customer in her store, saying that their Dad was doing something bad with Jeannie.

I talked to Faye and Elaine about this. They said they had heard grown-ups say this too.

"What does it mean?" we all said to each other. We thought maybe it meant what grow-ups do so that our Moms could have babies.

"But Jeannie's not a grown-up," we said.

I asked Mommy about it, and she said, "Ruthie, I think this is not our business,. It's gossip, and I don't want you talking about it."

She sounded very serious, so I didn't say anything more about it to anybody. But one day, I asked Georgie about it again. He pushed me down on the ground. "Shut up and leave me alone," he said and ran back into the school.

Sometimes I saw Jeannie in her yard if I rode my bike up to visit Virginia's house or the Scott's farm, or if someone drove us past in their car on the way to shop in Nipawin. Sometimes, if the weather was nice, I saw her outside with the baby. But I never talked to her, so I never knew anything about what happened.

Northern Lights

Sometimes in the winter, we would see something really beautiful happen in the sky. The adults called it "Northern Lights".

It only happened after it was dark out. Maybe I might be listening to the radio, or practicing the piano or reading a book. Then Mommy or Daddy would come in and say, "Come on outside. You kids just have to see this." Then we would all run outside and stand on the stones outside the back porch.

Up in the sky there were rows of colours. They weren't straight rows. They were moving up and down, and sometimes one colour seemed to go behind some of the other colours. Or sometimes one row of colours would move faster than the others. There were lots of colours, and they were shiny as they moved up and down. Their lines took up a big part of the sky. We could see some of them through the poplar trees and some others away up in the sky above the poplar trees.

We stood outside and watched the sparkling colours dancing in the sky. Sometimes, I would feel really cold, but I didn't want to go inside for my parka in case I missed some dancing lights. They didn't last for very long, but sometimes Mommy would go inside and bring our parkas out to me and Peter. "They are so beautiful," she would say, as we kept looking at the lights.

When we were back inside, Daddy told us, "We call them Northern Lights because nobody can see them further south. This only happens in the northern sky in Canada. And if it was snowing outside, we couldn't see the lights. Or if this was a cloudy night, we couldn't see them either. So we are the lucky people."

Other winter nights, the sky was clear but there were no dancing Northern Lights. Sometimes on those nights Daddy would take us out and show us some stars in the sky that looked like a big pot with a handle, and tell us that those stars were called the "Big Dipper". Then he showed us another bunch of stars called the "Little Dipper." He said we could even see those in the summer, as long as it was night time and there were no clouds in the dark sky. It was fun to look at those too, but I liked the dancing "Norther Lights" the most.

Mommy said she did too.

Piano Playing

We had a piano in the house in Garrick. It was standing against the wall in the living room, across from the chesterfield and the radio.

I took piano lessons from Mrs. Joseph, Artie's mom. She was my teacher in grade one too. She had a piano in her house, so I would walk across the road and down the lane, in the direction of the two schools, past Viola's trailer, but not as far as the Fong's house. Then I'd go and knock on the back door of the Joseph's house. Mrs. Joseph was always home when I got there.

When I first started the lessons, she showed me how to play the right notes from the books she had in her house. She would open the book and put it on the front part of the piano. Then she would show me how to pick the right piano key to match each note on the page. I was already in grade two in school when I started the piano, so I knew how to read. Picking the right piano keys to hit was sort of like reading. If you got the right notes from the sheet of music, the piano would play the song you wanted. But it was a lot slower than reading the words of a song from the blackboard at school or from the hymn book in Sunday school.

After a little while though, I got faster at reading the notes and hitting the right piano keys at the same time. Then I could hear that I was playing the song I wanted.

At first Mrs. Joseph let me take some of the music papers home. She and Mommy and Daddy called the papers "sheet music". Then I said I really liked playing the piano, and I wanted to take more lessons, so they ordered some sheet music for us. One day I went to the railway station with Daddy, and we picked it up from the train.

I was really excited because some of the new sheet music was songs that I liked on the radio. Then I could learn to play them myself. Then I tried singing the words I knew along with the song I was playing on the piano. That was really hard! But sometimes I got it right, and I could play and sing my song at the same time.

Mrs. Joseph was always nice, but some of the sheet music, or a book of music she gave me to practice was not songs I knew. It was little short tunes made for a person to practice playing with the right notes that were on the sheet music. She called this "music lessons", and she said that the more I practiced playing these, the better I would get, so that someday I could buy sheet music for all the songs I liked and then sing along as I played. I tried hard to practice a lot because I really wanted to do that.

I remembered that when we visited Yorkton, Babba and Dedda had a piano in their house too. Auntie Lydia played it a lot. She could sing when she played, and she sang a lot of songs from the radio.

I asked her once when she took piano lessons, and she said she never took any lessons. Mommy said that was called playing and singing "by ear". Auntie Lydia just knew how to do the right sounds without any lessons.

"I wish I could play and sing by ear," I said to Mommy.

"I can't do that either, sweetie," Mommy answered me. "Only a few people have really good ears for music. Lydia is one of those people. But she's downtown at work right now. You could go and practice on the piano. I've got a few things to do first, but when I'm done, you and Petey and I can go downtown and meet Lydia for lunch in that cafe on Broadway."

I was so excited to hear about going to the cafe that I ran right out into the living room to practice piano playing.

Watching
"The Wizard of Oz"

Even though there was no movie theater in Garrick, the adults would sometimes arrange to have a movie in the Legion Hall. Once we saw a movie starring a man named Bob Hope. He was pretty funny, but the grown-ups laughed a lot more than I did. Mommy and Daddy went too, and they took Peter and me, even though they worried that it cost money.

But the very best movie was "The Wizard of Oz". Mommy let me go with Dolores and Maureen. It cost ten cents for kids, but I said I had that much saved in my piggy bank that I kept in the orange box in my bedroom. When I told Mommy I had my own money, she gave me a big hug and said she would give me the dime.

"It's an important new movie," she said. "There's been a lot of advertising on the radio. So when you come home, you can tell us all about it."

Oh, I loved that movie so much. The scarecrow was my favorite character. But the movie was exciting from the very start, when the scarey tornado hit Kansas and blew Dorothy and three hired men away from her family's farm to the land of Oz.

The next day I told Mommy about the story in the movie. First I told her that the movie started in Kansas in black and white. The three hired men on the farm were in black and white, and so was a mean old lady on a bicycle. When they went to Oz, magic turned the movie all into colour. The three men turned into the Scarecrow, the Tin Man and the Cowardly Lion. They were Dorothy's friends and helped her find the Wizard.

The mean old lady turned out to be the bad witch, the Wicked Witch of the West. She was not good to Dorothy.

Mommy said she had never ever seen a movie that started in black and white and then switched to colour.

That summer we went to Yorkton. I made a discovery at the Yorkton library. I remembered the name of the man who wrote the book called "The Wizard of Oz" before they made it into a movie. His name was L. Frank Baum. I asked the the librarian if there was that book in the library. She was a very nice lady, and she found the book for me. But she was so nice that then she found two other stories by the same book writer, Mr. Baum. They were also about the land of Oz.

I was so excited. I was good at reading by then, and I spent days in that summer holiday reading those books about Dorothy and Oz. The two sisters, Carol and Doreen, who lived across the street from Babba and Dedda's house, liked the books too.

Then we heard that the Roxy Theatre in Yorkton was showing the movie. Mommy said that she liked the story I told her after I saw the movie in Garrick. She thought she would like to see it too.

"Oh, can I see it again?" I asked.

She said, "Yes, of course. It was you who told me the story, Ruthie."

Petey wanted to go too, so Mommy said she would take both of us. Then Carol and Doreen said they wanted to see it too, and their Mom gave them the money for the tickets. All four of us kids and our Mom went downtown to the Roxy one Saturday afternoon. So I got to see "The Wizard of Oz" two times in one summer.

Summer in Strongfield

One summer holiday, my Auntie Gwen, Daddy's sister, her husband Charlie Rannie and their son, John, came to visit us in Garrick. They had a car, and after a few days, of visiting, they took me with them when they drove down to visit Grannie and Grampa Woodward in Strongfield.

This time I visited Strongfield, it was not cold winter. It was summer, and it was nice and warm. But Grannie and Grampa didn't live in the big house that Daddy had grown up in any more. Grampa was still the post-master, and they lived in a house that was behind the post office. Their house and the post office were connected to each other.

Sometimes, if I was standing in the front of the post office, I would hear people asking Grampa if there was a letter for them. Sometimes he said "Yes", and would get it for them. Other times he would look in the box and say, "Sorry, there is nothing here for you today."

Maybe the person would then just say, "thank you" and leave the post office. Other times people might get upset. They would say things like, "Oh, my sister in Scotland is expecting a new baby. She said she would write and tell me as soon as it was born." Or maybe I would hear a big serious thing even, like "My brother in New Brunswick is really sick. I need to hear from my sister-in-law if he dies."

Grampa was a really nice man, so he would say things like telling them he was sorry about some of those serious things. I just stood there. I wouldn't say anything to grown-ups, but I might think "Why are they fussing like that? Grampa doesn't drive the train. He can't help it." But sometimes I felt sorry for them, like the lady who started to cry because her letter wasn't there.

The house behind the post office had two doors, one from the post office into the house. That was the living room where Grannie had the chesterfield with her crocheted doilies on its back and on its arms.

Then there was another door from the back yard behind the post office where Grannie and Grampa had their garden, and that door went into the kitchen Their bedroom was beside the living room, just behind the post office. There was a little bedroom just off the kitchen, kind of behind the stove, and that's where I stayed when I was there. In a summer when other cousins came to stay, like John and Dorothy Rannie, or Linda Woodward another year, one of them shared the bed with me and Grannie put some blankets and a pillow on the floor for the extra kid. Or sometimes it was me sleeping on the floor.

What ever it was, it was lots of fun sometimes. We got to see our cousins. We could walk around town and play with other kids, or we could walk across the tracks and pick berries in the bushes on the other side. Grannie and Grampa had a shelf full of books, and they weren't all only for grown-ups to read. One summer there was a fair that came for a few days in a field on the edge of town. It was like the fair we once had in Garrick, with a ferris wheel and places where you could buy candy and popcorn. If you could find some way to get the money! And if you helped Grannie with the dishes or the washing or weeding the garden, she might give you some money to buy a treat.

Drinks for Grown-ups

Sometimes I would hear the grown-ups talk about something called "prohibition". It sounded like it had something to do with drinking beer. Or maybe those other grown-up drinks in the bigger glass bottles that they sometimes called wine or gin or rye. Or maybe whiskey.

One summer day in Yorkton we were sitting in the car on Babba and Dedda's driveway. Uncle Walter was going to drive us somewhere, but he went back into the house to get something. So Mommy and Petey and Dedda and I were waiting in the car. Mommy said something to Dedda about building shelves. He talked about building many shelves in the houses he built.

But then he said to Mommy, "Way back in the days of Prohibition, I used to do work for that family we were talking about. They already had a house here in Yorkton, but they had storage sheds too. I used to do carpentry work for them. I built a lot of shelves in the sheds so they could store the bottles."

"They were the people who used to make liquor during Prohibition, weren't they?" said Mom.

"That was them," said Dedda. "I remember that it was once illegal to sell it in Canada, but I think it lasted a lot longer down in the States. I heard that was where they used to sell it."

"They still have a lot of silly rules about booze," said Mom. "You know Bert and I don't drink much, but when we go to a dance, we have to keep our bottle under the table. Lots of other people are doing that too. More people come to a dance with liquor than people who don't bring any. It's part of the evening out."

"Polya and I don't go to dances. That's for you younger people who grew up here in Canada." said Dedda. "But lots of people drank even when it was against the law here. That family made a lot of it, and it didn't sit around on those shelves for very long."

"Sometimes I used to help bottle it," he said. "I would fill up a bottle and tighten on the lid. Then I would slap on a label that said "Thirty-year Aged". And it was still warm."

He and Mommy both started laughing. Then Uncle Walter came out to the car, and we drove out of the driveway.

My friend from Carcross

One day when I was just starting grade two, I was looking in one of Daddy's papers, and I saw something about pen pals. It had names of different towns and then names of different girls who lived in those towns.

"What's a pen pal?" I said to Mommy.

"Oh," she said, "that's when you write to another girl, maybe somebody about your age, in another town, maybe in some other part of Canada. Then you two will get to know each other. Let's see what the paper says, Ruthie."

I handed her the paper, folded at the page I was looking at.

She read some of the names. "There's lots of them in Ontario," she said, "but that's really a different part of Canada than here in Saskatchewan."

Then she looked again and said, "And lots of these names are older than you. Some of them are grown-ups. Here's one that's twenty-seven. That wouldn't be any good for you."

"What would be good for me?" I said. "Would I write letters to this girl? What would I say?"

"Oh," said Mommy, "well, you know what you say when you write to Grannie Woodward. You tell her what you were learning in school and which friends you played with."

" I tell her what Daddy sold in the store, too," I said.

"That's because she's Daddy's mother," said Mommy. "But if you write to someone your age, you might talk more about what games you play with other kids or things like that."

"That sounds like fun," I said.

Then Mummy said, "What about the Yukon? It says there is a girl there who is eight. You are seven already, so you would be close in age."

"Where is Yukon?" I said.

"It's not a province," Mommy answered me. "It's like sort of something they call a territory of Canada. It's north of here, we are in the north part of Saskatchewan, so maybe you and this girl would have things to write about together."

"What's her name?" I said.

"Her name is Mary Conner, and she lives in Carcross, Yukon. Do you want to write her a letter?"

"What should I write?" I said.

"Well," said Mommy, "What about telling her about your school and what grade you're in. Tell her what kind of town Garrick is like. Or tell her about Peter and your baby sister. You can think about things, I bet."

"Is her address there?"

"Yes," said Mommy and she showed me the place in the paper with Mary's name and her post box number in this town called Carcross.

"I'll try it," I said, and Mommy helped me cut the name and address out of the page in the paper.

"Should I use pages from my scribbler?" I said.

"I could give you some of my writing paper," said Mommy, "but it isn't lined paper like in your scribbler. You just learned to print last year, so I think lined paper would be best. When you're finished the letter, we can cut the pages out of your scribbler, and mail the whole letter.

I was excited, so I got my scribbler out of my bedroom and sat down at the kitchen table with my pencil. I told Mary Conner about how I walked to school and what we were learning in grade two. I told her about my brother and sister and my friends Faye and Elaine.

When I thought the letter was long enough, Mommy helped me cut the pages out of my scribbler. I had written letters before, like to Grannie Woodward, so when Mommy got me an envelope, I knew how to print the address on the front and how to fold up the pages with the writing before I put them in the envelope and licked the back to glue it shut.

"Tomorrow," said Mommy, "we can go to the post office and buy a stamp. Do you have four cents?"

I went into my bedroom and looked into my piggy bank. I had eighteen cents. So I ran out to tell Mommy I was okay to buy the stamp.

She said that was good and clapped her hands. Then she said that she would give me the four cents to buy the stamp.

"It's your first pen pal," she said. "Maybe you can buy your own stamps if you keep writing to each other."

The next day she gave me the money and I went down the lane to the post office and bought the stamp. As I was pasting it on the front of the envelope, Mr. Wright said, "Carcross is a long way, Ruth."

"It's not as far as Ontario," I said to him as I gave him the letter to put in the mail.

Well, in two more weeks I got a letter back from Mary. She told me that she was in grade three, she told me about her school and about her Dad working in a garage and about her little sister who was five.

I wrote back, she wrote back, and we wrote to each other for a long time.

Viola In The Trailer

Linda was Faye and Elaine's cousin. She was in grade two when we were in grade three. Her mom's name was Viola, and she said she was Rosa Rutherford's sister.

Mrs. Rutherford said Viola was her younger sister. They had grown up together on a farm that was a long way north up the road that went past the schools.

Rosa said that there were eight kids in their family when they were little, but she and Viola were the only two still living in Garrick. Rosa once told me that two of her brothers had been killed in the war. Then she said that two other brothers had come home from the war. One time she told me that one of those brothers was now farming near Moose Jaw. I knew that Moose Jaw was farther south than Garrick, closer to Strongfield where Grannie and Grampa lived.

Rosa and Viola's parents still lived on the farm. I went there one time with Faye and Elaine and their family. They had a horse and wagon in their yard, and they had chickens, but there weren't any other farm animals.

Rosa's father was a mean old man. She had brought them a bag of potatoes and some other vegetables, and he yelled at her and said it wasn't enough. When he went outside, her mother thanked her. Her mother seemed like a nice old lady. But I was glad we didn't stay long.

Linda didn't have a father. She had a sister and two brothers and another brother who was just a little baby. They all lived with Viola in a trailer. The trailer was along the path that ran behind the Joseph's house, past the Fong's house and up to the schoolyard.

The trailer sat on four tires, and when you opened the front door to walk in, there was a driver's seat and a steering wheel like in the big bus we once took to go to Strongfield for Christmas. But there were no seats in the rest of the trailer.

There was a table and chairs along the wall under the window on the same side of the trailer as the steering wheel. Then there was a high chair sitting close to the table. Sometimes one of the kids younger than Linda sat in it.

Further back in the trailer, there was a wall with a door in it. Viola's bed was behind it, and there was a little dresser and a mirror on the wall and some hangars to hang clothes on. Then there was a smaller bed too. Maybe it was where Linda slept. I never asked her.

Back in the big part of the trailer there was another bed. It always had a blanket on it when I went over there. Like a couch, so we could sit on it.

I liked Viola. She was taller than Rosa, and she liked to talk to us if I came home with Linda. I thought she had very nice clothes, like a long blue skirt and one blouse with lace on the collar and sleeves. She had long dark brown curly hair, and one time I asked her if she used Toni permanents to curl her hair. She said, "yes", and then told me how she liked curly hair better than straight hair.

But Linda and her brothers and sister had no Dad living in the trailer. I wondered where he was, but I was afraid to ask Viola. That wasn't a question to ask a grown-up.

When I asked Linda she said she never had a Dad who lived in the trailer. She said she once asked her Mom. And Viola said he died a long time ago. That seemed very sad.

We came from very different kinds of families, but we kids were good friends with each other.

Fun at Sports Day

In the springtime, sometimes closer to summer, but before school was out for the year, the adults would organize a field day. Or some people called it Sports Day. The years I went, it was held in Choiceland.

I sometimes heard them talking about canceling the day if it rained, but I always remember nice sunny days.

Daddy had to find someone to drive us there. One year our family went in the back of Mr. Rutherford's truck. Another year, Mr. Emde drove a bunch of us kids on the back of his dray. That was lots of fun, but I think the parents must have got other rides that year.

When we got to Choiceland, we found the sports day in a big field on the edge of town. There were signs saying "Sports Day This Way", so you would know where to go.

There were booths set up where you could buy things like candies and popcorn and hot dogs. I always liked hot dogs, and as soon as we saw this booth, I asked Mommy if I could have one.

"Well, do you have your allowance with you, Ruthie? I see they cost 15 cents each."

"Oh," I said, "I already spent my allowance. You know I bought a Little Lulu comic book and some candy already."

Mommy laughed. "I know that. I was fooling. But later is when we can think about buying treats. First we want to see where the races are. And we should find out what times too. Don't you want to run in a race? Or do a high jump? You're good at those things."

"Oh yes," I said. "I forgot it was Sports Day. That's more fun than a hot dog."

We soon got to the field where they were having the races. There were ribbons and coloured tapes marking out the rows where the races were going to happen. And there were poles in some places to mark spots where people threw things or jumped over the poles. Then there were people sitting at different tables with signs saying which races and other sports. And the signs were saying the ages of the people for the different races.

Mommy and Daddy helped me find the right tables to sign up for races and high jumps for kids my age. When Petey was big enough, they helped him sign up for some races too.

Some kids were really really fast runners or really good at high jumping. But then when I ran, I came third in two different races. When the race was over, the grown-up running it lined up us kids who had won first, second and third, then she said our names out loud and gave us a coloured ribbon to pin on our blouses. After the sports day was over, I saved these ribbons at home in my orange-box cupboard in my bedroom. I was sad when I didn't win any high-jump ribbons. I couldn't get over the pole without knocking it down.

One time Petey won a race too, and he had a ribbon to bring home.

After the races were all over, we walked around the fields. We saw some some of the kids we knew from school, and some of them who didn't come into school much because their families needed them to work on their farms. And we met some new kids who lived in Choiceland. The adults walked around talking to each other too, and meeting new friends. Daddy was talking to other people from the stores in Choiceland about things they were selling and if they had a lot of customers. One year, Yvonne was there and she was talking to people from the stores too.

And after the races, Mommy did buy us hot dogs.

A Book And A Movie

There was a book in the school library called "Lassie Come Home". It was a story from some parts of England and Scotland. About a boy who had a dog named Lassie. He and his dog really loved each other. Then his parents needed some money, so they sold Lassie to another family who lived a long way away. But Lassie missed her boy, so the story was about a long, long trip she made back home, so they could be together again.

I loved the story when I read it, but then some of the adults brought the movie to the Legion Hall. I still loved the story, but the movie was in colour, and Lassie was a beautiful collie dog. She looked the same as the picture on the cover of the book I read, but I loved the beautiful collie dog in the movie even more.

So I asked Mommy and Daddy if we could get a dog, maybe a collie dog.

"Well, Ruthie," they said, "we don't really need a dog. People have dogs on their farms in case a wolf, or maybe a cayote, comes on the property and might try and grab a farm animal to eat."

"Lassie in the book was a nice dog. She loved the boy in the story. She wouldn't attack any other animals," I said.

"Well," Mommy said, "maybe in big cities, people have dogs for pets. Maybe they love each other But then you have to feed them. They're big animals. We couldn't afford to do that. It would be wasting too much money."

When Mommy started talking about wasting money, I knew I couldn't get her to change her mind.

"OK," I said, and I went out to play. Maybe, I thought, I could try another time to get one of those beautiful Lassie dogs.

My Favorite Kitty

Misty was a big fluffy gray kitty. Mommy said we needed her in the house to catch any mice that came in. I liked her to curl up beside me if I was reading a book on the chesterfield. If I patted her back, she would start purring. Sometimes she would sleep on the chesterfield at night, and sometimes in the daytime, she would sleep on the bottom bunk if Petey and I weren't playing there.

But mostly she slept in her own box that Mommy and Daddy had fixed for her in the corner of the kitchen, just across from the stove and behind the stool where Daddy kept his morning shaving stuff. The box had a little folded up piece of cloth from an old blanket in it. In the summer, Mummy put the box out on the back porch, because it was warm enough then.

Sometimes Misty had kitties. We would wake up in the morning to take her some food and find out that there were little kittens in the box with her.

The new baby kitties were very small, sometimes Misty had six of them. She would lay on her side, and they would suck on the little things on her stomach. Mommy told me these were called "teats". She said that mother cats, like Misty, would grow milk in their stomachs before the kitties were born, so that they could feed the kitties with the milk until the kitties grew bigger.

One thing we had to do was find people who wanted the new kitties. "We only need Misty to be in the house," Mommy said. One time I gave one kitty to Faye and Elaine because their old cat had died. They needed a new cat to go after the mice in their house. One time Charlie Fong took one for his store, and the people in the restaurant took two because they had mice trying to get into the food in their kitchen.

One spring something happened that I didn't like. All six of the new kitties were gone. Mommy and Daddy told me that someone on a farm had needed all six of them at once. But a few days later, I was wading in the water in the ditch in front of our house. I thought I stepped on something. So I stopped to reach down to see what it was. I pulled it up. It was a mesh bag full of dead baby kitties.

I picked it up and ran into the house. It was a Sunday, and Daddy was home reading the paper and Mommy was peeling potatoes for supper.

I was crying and holding up the dripping wet bag full of dead baby kitties.

"What happened to my poor little kitties?" I asked, as I cried some more.

Daddy came into the kitchen. He and Mommy looked at each other for a minute. Then Daddy said, "We don't want to lie to you, Ruthie. We think you're old enough to know. We try to give the baby kitties away. You know that. But sometimes everybody has enough cats, and no one takes them. Like this spring. We only need Misty in the house. So I drowned those kitties in the ditch. Lots of people do that when they have too many."

He took the dripping bag of dead kitties off the floor and tried to hug me. Mommy came and hugged me too. I kept crying, but they kept saying how they didn't want to hurt me and how we still had Misty.

Then Misty saw us and came over and rubbed against us. I hugged her and tried to stop crying. Mommy asked if I would like to have some rice pudding, even before supper and dessert. Soon things were better. I never found any more dead kitties. But I sometimes wondered if Daddy had drowned them in a place I didn't know about.

Not long after that, in the summer time, something else happened to Misty. She came into the back porch one afternoon with her two back legs dragging behind her. She was meowing a lot.

"Oh my God," said Mommy. She let Misty go into the kitchen, then she brought her box in from the porch and put a clean tea towel into the box and put Misty in on top of it.

"There, there," Mommy was saying as she patted her, then she asked me to sit beside Misty's box. She warmed up another tea towel in front of the stove, and we put it on top of her.

I sat there with Misty for a long time, patting her and talking quietly to her. She meowed for a long time, but then she stopped. We kept covering her with warm towels until I went to bed. The next morning she was still lying in the box. She didn't even try to get up.

A few days later, when Daddy came home from the store for supper, he told us that a farmer had come into the store and told him how Misty had been run over by a tractor. "He told me," Daddy said, "that she had been running across the street under the tractor and just didn't quite make it before the back wheel of the tractor ran over her back legs." The farmer said the guy on the tractor didn't even see her, so he just drove on. And then the farmer didn't even come and tell anybody because he said, "I thought that cat was a dead one for sure." Then he told Daddy that someone in town had said the crazy old cat was still alive. "So then," said Daddy, "he decided to come and tell me how the cat had got run over."

Now we knew what had happened to poor Misty. For a long time after that, she was just lying in the box in the kitchen. We were feeding her and patting her and covering her with warm blankets. Petey was helping too. I think she couldn't walk on her back feet. Maybe it was like when a person had a broken foot. Except you didn't put one of those white casts on a kitty.

But before the end of summer, before I went back to school, Misty got up out of her box and started walking. Soon she was walking pretty fast, and by the time it snowed, in the fall, she was running again.

But the next spring, she only had three kitties.

Starting Grade One

Faye and Elaine and I all started grade one at the same time. Before school started Daddy brought me home two scribblers and two pencils from his store. The scribblers had pages inside them with lines on them. Mommy and Daddy said those lines would be good when I learned how to print words.

"Won't I learn how to write too?" I asked.

They told me that printing came first, along with learning to read. Writing would happen in grade two, or maybe grade three.

I had seen some scribblers with pictures on the covers that you opened to get to the lined pages inside. But my scribblers had plain covers with only a few words. I asked what the words said, and Mommy laughed and told me that I would find out when I learned to read.

"And can Daddy get out his knife and sharpen the pencils for me?" I asked.

"No," said Daddy. "They have something in the school called a pencil sharpener. That will be more fun for you to use."

The day before the first day of school it was raining. It stopped by the next morning, but the road up to the school was all muddy, so Mr. Rutherford drove us up there in his truck. He stopped on the road just beside the little bridge that crossed the ditch beside the road and went into the schoolyard. When I got out of the truck, my shoes got muddy. So did Faye's and Elaine's shoes. But when we got to the school steps, we found there was a scraper at the top of the steps, just outside the door.

So we scraped our shoes, and went though the door into the school building. There was a little space inside with hangars all along the walls.

But we didn't need winter coats in September, so we didn't have anything to hang. Then we went through the door right into the big school room. The first thing I saw was the blackboard at the other end of the room. Mrs. Joseph was already standing behind her desk in front of the blackboard.

I knew that Mrs. Joseph was a very nice lady. She was my friend Arty's mother, and Arty was already in school in Grade Two. He was the youngest in their family, and he had some older brothers and sisters. Some of them had already moved away from Garrick. Mr. Joseph ran one of the town elevators down by the railroad tracks.

Some kids were already there in school. There was the row of windows along the side wall. Those kids were sitting in desks in rows in front of Mrs. Joseph.

"You three girls are in grade one," said Mrs.

Our Grade One class
on the steps of the school

Joseph when we came in. "That is the row beside the window there." And she walked over to three desks and told us where to sit. "These will be your desks until I might tell you to move later."

I sat down in my desk. It had a little table right in front of me and a drawer under the seat. I put my scribblers in the drawer. Elaine was second in the row by the window, I was behind her, and Faye was behind me.

"I need to sharpen my pencils," I said to Mrs. Joseph.

"Well, Ruth," she said, "There is a pencil sharpener right here." She was standing a little behind me, near where Faye was sitting, and she pointed to the funny thing stuck onto a shelf near the windowsill.

"Bring your pencils here," she said, so I took them over to her.

The thing on the shelf had a handle and a hole on the other side from the handle. She showed me how to put my pencil in the hole and then turn the handle. After a few turns, she said, "Now stop turning, and pull out the pencil." I did that, and I saw that the pencil now had a pointed end, all ready for printing.

"Now that you know how it works, you can sharpen your other pencil," said Mrs. Joseph. "You can sharpen them whenever you have to. But not when I'm teaching the class. You'll learn lots of good new things, Ruth."

Next she showed me the rows of boxes under the windowsill. There were three rows of them, and some had books and other stuff in them. She pointed to a box in the bottom row and said, "This is your box. These are for you kids to keep your own things in. You can keep your sandwich there too, if you don't go home to eat at noon time."

Then she pointed across the room and said, "See those shelves beside the wall, past the grade three desks." I looked and saw a cupboard with books on all its shelves. "That's our school library," Mrs. Joseph said. "If you find a book you like, you can take it home. You just have to tell me first, and I will write your name down and tell you what day you have to bring it back." I could hardly wait to see a bunch of new books.

She told me there were twelve new kids starting grade one that day, so she had to go and help some other kids, so I sharpened my second pencil and went to sit in my own desk. I liked it. I had my own drawer under my seat and a piece of wood to lean my arm on and reach over to the front of the desk. There was a little kind of table top there, so I could put my scribblers on it to print. It was going to be fun to learn that.

Then there was the stove at the back of the room. It wasn't burning today because it wasn't cold out, but there was a pile of wood behind the stove against the back wall. It looked like the pieces of wood Daddy kept on the back porch and the kitchen to put in the stoves in our house in the winter time.

The stove was an oil barrel with four metal legs holding it up. It had the door in the front, and then the chimney went up and through a hole in the roof.

More and more kids were coming into the school now, so I pulled one of my scribblers and one pencil out of my drawer, and looked up at Mrs. Joseph. Then I turned back to Faye and said, "We're starting school."

The Smith Family

Yvonne worked in Daddy's store. Most of the time she was behind the counter, selling things to people and taking their money to put in the cash register. Sometimes she helped Daddy take things out of boxes, at the back of the store and put them on the shelves for people to look at. One time I watched her help Daddy put some things on the shelf in front of the window, so people could look in from the sidewalk and maybe see things they wanted to come in and buy.

Yvonne had red hair. She was a grown-up, but not very old, and she was always nice to me. Sometimes she would make a face, just for fun, and push her teeth out in front of her lips and wiggle them back and forth. She said she could move them like that because they were false teeth. "The first summer we came up to Garrick, our family didn't have any money, so all we had to eat that summer were saskatoon berries. So my teeth weren't very healthy. Then when I got older, I had to go to Nipawin, and a dentist took them all out and put in the false teeth." That's what she told me one day.

Her Mom and Dad were Mr. and Mrs. Smith who had the hotel when we first moved to Garrick. They had those kind of accents that people who came from England had. It was sort of like Grannie and Grampa Woodward, but more. I heard Mr. Smith telling some other grown-ups that one time he had a farm in southern Saskatchewan, near where Regina is. Then he said that this thing adults sometimes called "the Depression" came along, and his grain didn't grow. He said, "I came up to Garrick with five dollars in my pocket and two good horses." I never heard what happened to the horses.

Yvonne said they had farmland around the road to Nipawin, but nobody was living on it now. That was where they were living in the summer when they ate the saskatoon berries. Then her parents started running the hotel.

She also said she had two brothers. They were older than her, and they were not in Garrick because they were in the army. She said they had both been in Europe fighting in the same war that Connie Mae's Dad had been in, the one the adults called World War Two.

One day Yvonne's brothers came to Garrick. She said they might be taking the farmland. She went out of town one day with her brothers and Mr. Smith. They did that a few times, then Yvonne told me that the whole family was going to move out there and start farming, as soon as her parents found someone else to run the hotel. Soon the Sullivan family moved into the hotel, and Yvonne and Mr. and Mrs. Smith moved out to the farm.

I saw her sometimes when the family came into town. Daddy didn't get a new person for the store, so he was at the front counter and the till most of the time. Sometimes he let me help him unpack things and put them on the shelves. I liked helping. I thought maybe one day he might teach me how to put the money in the till.

I never found out if Mr. Smith got any new horses.

What About Mom and Dad?

One cloudy summer afternoon I was walking down the lane from our house to the main street sidewalk between the post office and Daddy"s store. Then Larry Rutherford came off their back porch and started walking down the lane ahead of me.

"Hey, Larry," I shouted, but he didn't answer me. He looked mad, and he was walking pretty fast with his head down. I tried to catch up with him, but pretty soon he was at the wooden sidewalk where it crossed the lane. I saw him stop and look around. When I got to the sidewalk he was in the middle of the road talking to a man who was just tying his horse to one of the poles beside the field on the other side of the road.

"What?" said the man he was talking to, and Larry talked to him some more. They went across the street to another man who was standing on the sidewalk and they started talking. Then another man came out of the post office and talked to them. Then all three men started laughing.

By then I was standing on the road close to all of them. I heard Larry saying, "But my Dad was hurting my Mom." The men started laughing again. Larry started crying. "He just came home from the garage, and he's hurting Mommy. She's shouting."

The men started laughing again, but then Mr. Smith came along the sidewalk. All the men laughed again and talked to Mr. Smith. Then he turned around and said to Larry, "Why don't you come over to the hotel with me, Larry. I think I've got some candy, and you can talk to me for a little while. Then you can go home. Your Mom is going to be okay."

I wished Mr. Smith could give me some candy, but I was afraid to ask. Larry stopped crying and went to the hotel. The men kept laughing. They were using that swear-word we were told to never ever use. They were saying things like, "I hope Bob's having a good one."

I didn't know why the men were laughing. So I went across the street and started swinging.

Washing and Ironing

Sometimes on Monday, the day when Mommy always did the washing, it would all dry really fast. That was on nice summer days. Sometimes, when I came home from school, she already had it off the clotheslines. Sometimes nice fall days and spring days were like that too.

But some days it was raining. Once I said to Mommy, "Why don't you do the washing tomorrow? Or some other nice day?"

She said, "It has to be organized. We only have so many clothes. Daddy needs to have clean shirts to wear in the store. What if I did it, and you didn't have a blouse to wear to school because it was dirty? Or no clean underpants?"

"Yuk," I thought, and I didn't ask her about that any more.

Some of those rainy days there were wet clothes, sheets or tea towels hanging on the backs of our kitchen chairs or from the end of my top bunk. But Mommy had a wooden thing in the back porch too. If it was raining she brought it out into the kitchen and unfolded it. Then it stood up with a bunch of rows and bars for hanging clothes on. Sort of like a big triangle. If it was winter, she put it on the kitchen floor in front of the stove and opened the oven door. She said all that heat dried the washing.

Once things were dry, lots of them needed ironing. Mommy had two irons made out of metal. They were called "sad" irons. I thought that was funny. How could a thing like an iron be sad? "Sad" was for people. Mommy laughed when I said that. The irons were shaped with a point at one end that curved out to the back end. The back end was flat, not pointed.

Each iron had a handle. The handles were made of wood and fit into a person's hand so they could hold it. The other end of the handle had a little moving screw that hooked it onto the top of the metal part.

Mommy heated up the metal part on the top of the stove. Even in summer she had to have a fire to heat up the irons. When the bottom was hot, she hooked the wooden handle onto the metal bottom part, and the iron was ready to go.

Some ladies had ironing boards, but Mommy ironed on the kitchen table. She pulled it away from the window so it was more in the kitchen, then she put a big piece of folded cloth on the table. She called that her "ironing pad". Then she took turns with putting the things she wanted ironed on the pad and ironed them with the hot iron. When she was using one iron, the other one was getting hot on the top of the stove.

I used to hear the grown-up ladies talking about ironing sometimes. Some of them said that other ladies did too much. They said jeans and other pants that kids played in didn't need ironing. They only got dirty anyway. Some ladies said you should only iron clothes that you wore to dress up in, like to go to church on Sunday, or to a dance or to go to Nipawin. But they all argued about ironing sheets. Some said that was really, really stupid because people just slept on them and they got all wrinkled right away. Other ladies said it was important for the "household". It should be "well cared for".

Mommy ironed our sheets except on days when the wet, cold laundry hung up in the house for two or three days before it dried. If the sheets took that long she might just fold them and put them away without ironing.

Sometimes she let me try ironing something, like maybe some tea towels. But I liked it best when she let me iron my school blouse. The iron was pretty heavy, and she said I should be very careful not to burn my hands, and she watched me do it. I liked ironing. It was fun. I thought I could do more when I grew bigger. Even sheets.

I Learn About Rent

When we visited Babba and Dedda in Yorkton after they moved to the big new house on Second Avenue South, there were two ways to go downtown to Broadway Avenue. The first way was to walk down Tupper Avenue. Auntie Lydia walked along Tupper to go downtown to her work in an office in the mornings during the week.

I didn't do that. But sometimes during the days I walked down with Babba to collect money. The houses we went to were on both sides of Tupper Avenue. Babba told me that theses were houses that Dedda had built. She told me the money was something called "rent".

"Well, you know, Ruthie, because Dedda built the house, it is our house. But we don't want to live in it." She smiled at me. Babba didn't laugh much, but she smiled when she said, "We couldn't live in more than one house, could we?"

"No. That would be silly," I answered, as we walked up the sidewalk and knocked on the door of one of the houses. A lady answered the door.

"Good morning, Mrs. Katelnikoff," she said, "I guess you're coming for the August rent."

"Good morning, Mrs. Martin," said Babba, as the lady handed her an envelope with some letters and numbers written on the front. Babba opened the envelope and pulled out some bills. She counted them and then put the envelope in her pocket and took out a piece of paper. She gave the piece of paper to Mrs. Martin. They both said "thank you" and wished each other a happy day. Then Babba and I walked down the sidewalk and back along Tupper Avenue to another house.

"What's the piece of paper for, Babba?" I said.

"Dedda calls it a receipt, Ruthie," she said. "He is the one who always talks to the people when they rent the houses. Well, he and the men always talk and agree on how much rent they will pay to live in the house. They pay the rent at the start of each month. Sometimes Dedda comes to collect it, but, like today, he is working on another house, so I go and collect it. He tells me how much it is and writes it on the receipt. Did you see I counted the lady's money before I gave her the paper receipt?"

"Yes, I saw you do that." I said.

"So," said Babba, "if they paid me the right amount, I gave them the receipt. That proves they paid this month's rent. And when I get home, Dedda writes the amount in the book where he lists the rents we collect."

"What if they don't give you the right amount of money?" I asked.

"Well," said Babba, "I might count it two times. But I have to tell them it's the wrong amount. I can only give them the receipt if it's the right amount written on it. Most the time, if it's a mistake, we figure it out."

"What if you don't figure it out?" I asked.

"Then I don't give them the paper, and I tell them that Mr. Katelnikoff will be down to solve the problem." She smiled again. "They always pay the right amount then."

By now we were walking up to the next house, and I walked along with Babba. I never saw anybody pay the wrong rent on any of my summer holidays.

A Choir in Canada

One day I was sitting in the back seat of a car. We were driving somewhere from Strongfield. Grannie and Auntie Gwen were sitting and talking in the front seat. But it wasn't my Auntie Gwen, Daddy's sister, it was Grannie's sister. Her name was Gwen too, but her name was Gwen Foster. She was visiting Grannie and Grampa in Strongfield. One day Auntie Gwen told me that she grew up in Bath, in England, just like Grannie did.

"She's my older sister," she said. "Then your Grannie married Reg Woodward. He was a schoolteacher who came from Yorkshire, not Bath."

"I know that," I said. "Grannie told me that Grampa taught school here in Saskatchewan once too. It was in a town called Loreburn. Then he thought the farm boys who came in to school were too tough, so he came here to Strongfield to be the postmaster instead."

"But Ruthie," said Auntie Gwen," Did you know that your Grannie went back to England once."

"No," I said, "I didn't know that. When did she go there?"

"She did it when Gwen, your auntie, not me, was just a little baby. She came back to Bath and stayed with our parents. She was there for quite a few months. She was already expecting your Auntie Louise. Did you know Louise was born in England?"

"No, I didn't know that," I said.

"Well, you see, you know your Auntie Nancy and Auntie Gwen are both about the same age, and so are your Auntie Una and Auntie Louise."

I knew both those aunties a little bit from visiting them. We had been to see Auntie Nancy on her and Uncle Wilmer's farm one summer. Auntie Gwen lived with them.

"But what your Grannie wanted to do in England was to talk me and Mr. Foster into coming to Canada." She started laughing. She and I were always close as sisters when we grew up. I missed her, and I kind of liked the idea of trying to live in Canada. But my husband, Mr. Foster, was a choir master in Bath. He right away said to Nan, your Grannie, "Do they have many choirs on those Saskatchewan prairies?"

Nan's answer was, "We have a very nice church in Strongfield. It would be lovely if someone started a choir.

"She kept making that argument to my husband. Then she would tell him about other things they liked to do. And she would tell him how much Reg, your Grampa, really liked Saskatchewan. And that was true, Ruthie. He has always been happy in Strongfield."

"Grampa's always happy," I said. "He's a really nice man. He never gets mad at anybody or yells. Some men yell a lot," I said. Then I asked her, "What happened to Mr. Foster?"

"Well, Ruthie," she said, "You know he died before you were born. He was also a very nice man, and I've missed him a lot. But we did come out to Saskatchewan. Your Auntie Nancy was a baby then. Mr. Foster tried to organize a choir in Strongfield. But there weren't enough people in town who wanted to join a choir. For a while he worked in the lumberyard and tried to organize singing in the church on some Sundays.

"Then someone told him about a church in Calgary that wanted to start a choir. For a few years we lived in Calgary. The choir did get started. Your Auntie Una was born in Calgary. But after a few years the choir just didn't grow. People here on the prairies have too much work to do. We like to sit and sing sometimes, but the regular practices for a good choir just take more time than people have to spare from work and farming and driving into town.

"So Mr. Foster started working for an insurance company and doing some small jobs for a couple of well-off men who were involved with the church. I think they wanted to help him keep trying to organize a choir in their church. Then one winter he got very sick, and he died in the spring. The doctor in the hospital called it cancer and said there was no way to cure it. By then Nancy was married and they took me to live with them on their farm."

"That was so sad," I said. "It was," said Auntie Gwen. Then she went back to talking to Grannie about how they could find a Protestant minister to come and give a sermon in the church in Strongfield.

My Family of Cousins

One summer our cousins came and visited us in Garrick. Uncle Jack, Daddy's brother was their Dad. Uncle Jack was an engineer. Daddy told me that he had gone to university in Vancouver to study engineering. And then he had been in the Navy for a while.

There were four kids in the family. Michael was the oldest boy. He was two years older than I was. Jimmy, the second brother, was born in the same year as I was, but I was three months older. Alan, the third brother, was younger than Jimmy, and Linda, the only girl in the family, was just four. They had an older boy, named John, traveling with them. He had been living with relatives, and was now going back to his parents.

I thought Auntie Helen was a beautiful lady. She had long dark hair like some of the movie stars. I asked her if she ever did a Toni permanent, and she said "no". She said she liked her hair long and straight because it looked better than "fake curls."

The family was moving to a place called Port Hope, Ontario because Uncle Jack had a new job there. He also had a car. They had been driving from Vancouver. I heard the adults talking about what a long trip it was. Then they talked about how it had been such a long time since Daddy and Uncle Jack had had a chance to visit with each other.

They liked to talk about how much fun they had playing outside together when they were little boys in Strongfield.

Uncle Jack told one story that made me laugh. The school he and Daddy went to in Strongfield sounded a lot like our school in Garrick, with one room for a bunch of grades. All the teachers were ladies. One day the teacher was mad at one boy. She called him up to the front of the room. It must have been about his work because she picked up a pile of papers from her desk and started waving the papers in his face and yelling at him. All of a sudden the papers flew out of her hand and all over the schoolroom floor.

The teacher kept yelling at the boy standing in front of her and didn't do anything about the papers. While she was yelling at the one boy, all the other kids sat quietly in their desks, hoping she wouldn't get mad at them.

Except for young Bert, my Dad. He said that he got out of his desk and went between the rows of seats and picked up all the papers on the floor. Then he put them into a nice neat pile.

"I sure remember what happened next," laughed Uncle Jack.

Soon the teacher stopped yelling and told the other boy to go back to his desk and sit down. Then Bert walked up to the front of her desk and held out the nice neat pile of paper to the teacher. He said in a very polite voice, "You dropped your papers, Miss Johnson." Daddy never said what happened next. But Uncle Jack started laughing. "I remember we all thought she looked really stupid. Then I was afraid you'd be the one to get in real trouble. Get the strap maybe. But she just pretended everything was okay. She took the papers quietly and just said, "Thank you, Bert. You go and sit down now." She never talked about it again, but we all laughed at her after school."

He and Uncle Jack also talked about catching gophers in the fields outside of Strongfield. They said there was a government plan to get rid of gophers, and kids could get a nickel if they handed in dead gopher's bodies.

When we kids went to bed at night the adults got out some extra blankets from our house and some that Uncle Jack and Auntie Helen had brought in their car. They put them on the floor for the kids to sleep on. The older boy, John, got a blanket on the floor beside Petey's and my bunk bed and Linda got to sleep with me in the top bunk. We were all glad it was summer, so it was not so cold that we needed a lot more blankets.

After we all went to bed, the adults brought the kitchen lamp out into the living room with the living room lamp, and sat for a long time and talked to each other about Uncle Jack's new job and about my aunts and uncles and other people they knew.

They were also talking about how Grannie and Grampa had saved up enough money to give every one of their children one hundred dollars when they finished high school. It was so they could leave home or do more education or get set up in their grown-up life. Daddy said it had been enough for him to go to Regina and rent a room in a house, where the landlady served supper, and also go to business school to learn bookkeeping and then get a job as a bookkeeper at Smith Fruit. Uncle Jack said it was not enough for him to finish university for all of his engineering training, but that he got started and after that he was working part time, so he could finish. Then he had joined the Navy. But he said he was doing work in Canada, not what they called "overseas", like when adults talked about Connie Mae's father in Strasbourg.

I was glad it was summer because in the daytime Petey and I went out to play with all the cousins and John. We went and found our other friends and ran to the swings in the field and over to the railroad tracks, then over to Ronnie Emde's Dad's barn and then up the road to the two schools. The school doors were locked for the summer, but there was lots of room to play in the yards and climb the trees beside them.

We had two days to play together, then Uncle Jack's family had to load up their car and their little trailer to keep on driving to Ontario.

A little while later Daddy got a letter from his brother saying that they had got to Port Hope and found a house to live in, and that he was working at his new job.

Daddy gave me the new address from the letter and I wrote a letter to my cousin, Michael, because he was the oldest. And he wrote me back. It was fun to get to know my cousins.

Stories From
Book of the Month Club

Some of the books Daddy got from the Book of the Month Club weren't just for grown-ups. There were books with stories for us kids too. Petey and I would sit beside him on the chesterfield some nights and he would read to us. "Heidi" was my first favorite book. It was about a little girl who lived in some mountains in a place called Switzerland. We didn't have any mountains in Garrick. I asked Daddy where this place called Switzerland was. He stopped reading and went and got his map from the shelves in his and Mommy's bedroom. I'd seen the map before when he showed me where England was, because Grannie and Grampa were born there. And he showed me Russia where Dedda and Babba came to Canada from. Switzerland was sort of in the middle of these two, a long way from Canada. Now I knew about another country in the world, and I loved the little girl, Heidi. The writer of the book was a lady, and her name was Johanna Spyri. I liked the sound of that name when Daddy told it to me.

Then I learned about another country in the world called India. That was in a book called "Kim". That was the name of a tough young boy growing up as an orphan on the streets in India. When Daddy showed me India on the map I could see it was a really long way from Canada.

"Daddy knows about India because the English run it," said Mommy with a laugh from the kitchen, where she was cleaning up after supper.

"Well, the Russians would do it if they could," Daddy laughed back. Then he went on reading to us about Kim, and his adventures as he was growing up.

The man who wrote the book was named Rudyard Kipling. He also wrote a set of two books called "The Jungle Books" that Daddy got for us. The main person in those stories was a boy called Mowgli. But he was more like some of his animal friends than he was like a person. His friends were Shere Khan, who was a tiger and Baloo, who was a bear. I always liked Baloo the best. They all had adventures together that were sort of like things that people might do. But their adventures were in far away places like jungles, not in towns like Garrick.

Then Daddy did buy a book that had places in Canada in it. The name of the book was "Flint and Feather", by a woman called E. Pauline Johnson. It was all poems. Some of them talked about places in Canada, like New Brunswick or Cyprus Hills or Brandon. Or Thunder Bay on Lake Superior. Some of the poems talked about grain growing on the prairies, like what farmers around Garrick did. My favorite poem was called "The Song My Paddle Sings". We even read that one in school. I loved poems. Sometimes I even made up some poems myself. It was fun to get two lines to rhyme.

By the time we ordered "Alice in Wonderland", I could read by myself. I was in grade two. Daddy asked if I wanted him to stop reading to me. I said "no". I liked my own reading and the books from the school library. But I still loved to curl up beside Petey and listen to Daddy read a story.

Comic Books and Candy

My allowance every week was fifteen cents. Petey got ten cents because he was younger. When I asked Mommy what I could use it for, she said it was okay to buy candy. My favorite chocolate bar, Neilson's, cost seven cents, and I liked buying those. A bottle of Coke was seven cents too.

Mommy also told me I could buy comic books with my allowance, and my most favorite thing to buy was a Little Lulu comic. They cost ten cents. That was a big part of my allowance, but they only came out once a month.

I loved the stories and the drawings. Little Lulu was a girl, and she was always laughing and teasing her friends. I liked her curly hair and her red dresses. There was always a new story or something happening to her or the other kids.

I also liked Superman comics, even if some kids said they were more for boys. They were about adventures in big cities and fighting against bad people. One thing I liked about Superman was his uniform. The comic would start about this sort of boring man in an office. His name was Clark Kent, and he had a girl friend named Lois Lane. The paper he worked for was called the Daily Planet, and that made me think he sounded as if something exciting was happening even when he wasn't Superman. Then, when something bad happened he magically turned into Superman. He had a coloured costume and he could fly through the air and jump over buildings to catch the bad guys. Sometimes I bought a Marvel comic book. The heroes in those comics fought bad guys too. Sometimes the Marvel drawings had really good bright colours, and I liked that. But I liked Superman better. I liked his costume, and he seemed more like a real person, sort of happy or funny sometimes.

I didn't have a big enough allowance though to buy too many comics every month, and get my chocolate bars and bubble gum too. And Little Lulu was still my favorite.

Recess Games

We had recess in school two times a day, fifteen minutes in the morning and fifteen minutes in the afternoon. When the time was up, Mrs. Joseph or Miss Zeorb would ring the bell so we would know that we should come back into the school. Sometimes, when it was really really cold in the winter, recess would be canceled, and maybe in the summer if it was raining hard. On days we couldn't go outside, most the time the whole class would sing. But recess was usually what happened. In good weather, especially in summer, we played games in the schoolyard. One of them was called "Red Rover." We would stand in two rows with the same number of kids on each side. Then we would pick one side to start, and that side would pick somebody from the other side. If it was, maybe Maureen, then our side would all sing, "Red Rover, Red Rover, we call Maureen over". Then she had to get over to our side and grab our hands so that we couldn't hold hands any more. If she stopped us from holding hands, she could take more people over to her side. If we stopped her from breaking us up, she had to stay with us. We played until one side had no one left. Or maybe the game ended when the teacher rang the bell.

Another game was called "A Tisket, A Tasket". We would all get in a circle. Then one person was picked to take a handkerchief. Sometimes one of us kids had one, but there were some cloth handkerchiefs in a bag on a hook near the stove in the school. Then we sang the song, "A Tisket, a tasket, a green and yellow basket, I wrote a letter to my Mom and on the way I dropped it. My little brother picked it up and put it in his pocket." When we got to that part of the song, the person with the handkerchief dropped it behind somebody. That person had to grab the handkerchief and run around the circle after the person who had dropped the handkerchief. When the kid who had dropped the handkerchief got caught they had to get back in the circle. Then the person who had caught them had to run around with the handkerchief until the song was over again and they dropped it behind another person who had to pick it up and try and catch the kid who dropped it.

I always liked playing those games.

Electric Lights

One summer, an aunt and uncle and their family came to visit the Scott family. Donny and Denny and their cousin came into town from their farm one afternoon. The cousin said he came from a town further south in Saskatchewan. I think it was close to Regina.

We were walking across the field to the railroad tracks, and the cousin said, "You guys don't have electricity in Garrick yet."

We knew that. So we said, "Do you have it?"

"Yes", he said, "We got it last year. It was really exciting."

"How exciting?" we asked him. "We're okay without it."

Peter Woodward and Donny Scott both turned 6 in September. Mommy and Mrs. Scott made a cake for them just near the Scott's farm.

"Well," he said, "We heard it was coming before it happened. We thought we were okay too. But I got home from school one afternoon, and my mother pointed to the light switch in the living room, and she told me to turn it on." He waved his hands in front of our faces as he talked. "Wow," he shouted. "a single light bulb on the ceiling in the middle of the room came on. I'll never forget that moment. It was so exciting. Strange, new, but very exciting."

"Well, the light comes on when we bring the coal oil lamp into the living room too," I said back to him.

"Well, you'll be excited too when you get electricity here in Garrick," he answered, as we kept on across the grass to walk on the railroad tracks.

Daddy's Kodak Camera

Daddy had a camera, and he really liked it. He called it a Brownie camera, and he said it was made by a company called Kodak. When he wanted to take a picture he pressed a button that made the glass at the front of the camera move out at the end of a black piece that looked like it had all been squeezed together before it came out. Then after he took the picture and pressed the button again to turn the camera off, the black piece went back into the camera.

He didn't have a camera before we moved to Garrick. I don't remember if it came on the train to Garrick or if maybe he bought it in Prince Albert before we moved. After we got to Garrick, he took a picture of Petey and me in front of the hotel where we were staying when they built the kitchen on our house. Then he took another picture of us sitting on the front steps of his new store. One winter day when I was in grade two, he took a picture of a bunch of us kids playing in the snow out near Mr. Schindel's farm. Then he told us it was time to go home, so we all walked back to our house with him. Because it was winter, the oil barrel that Mommy kept under the eaves trough at the corner of the kitchen could not catch rain water in the winter, so the barrel was lying in the back yard between the poplar trees. In one picture Petey and Ronny and Denny were sitting on the oil barrel and Faye and I were on the ground beside the barrel. Then he took another picture of Petey standing on the oil barrel and hanging onto the branch of one of the poplar trees behind the barrel. You could see lots of snow behind us in those pictures and all of us kids were wearing our winter parkas.

One day in the summer, he came out of the store and brought his camera over to the town swings. Yvonne was in the store in case there were customers. Daddy took a picture of me and Petey together sitting on the swings. Then he was going to take another picture of all of us kids who were standing there. Maureen jumped onto the swing really fast, and Petey and I and Delores were standing beside her. In the back of one of the pictures, you could see the elevators away down the railway tracks.

One summer day, Faye and Elaine and Maureen and I were playing on the wooden sidewalk, just before the lane that went between the post office and Daddy's store. It was a really hot sunny day, so Faye and Elaine and I were only wearing our sunsuits and bare feet. Maureen had a dress on and her shoes, so maybe she was going somewhere later.

Ruth, Maureen, Elaine and Faye on a summer day in front of the Post Office. Mr. Mitchells' store is down the sidewalk. Some of the windows of the hotel across the road show in the picture.

Daddy came out of the store with his camera. He laughed and said he wanted us to all line up in a row on the sidewalk so he could take a picture. We all lined up in a row, and when Daddy said "smile", we all smiled. When he showed me that picture later, you could see us girls all together on the sidewalk beside the post office. It showed the big summer vine climbing up beside the post office door, then the fence of the old lady's house between there and Mr. Mitchell's store. Maureen's family lived there above the store, on the top floor. At the end you could see a little corner of the hotel across from the end of the wooden sidewalk. That was one of my favorite pictures.

I loved looking at the pictures that Daddy took. It was like you could see yourself, and it reminded me of fun things we had done. But Daddy said it was expensive to take too many pictures. He said the film had a number, like 120, and that he had to order it from somewhere. Then he said that each film cost one dollar, and that it cost more to get the pictures on the film developed and sent back to Garrick. I was still glad he took the pictures. And he always let me look at them if I sat at the kitchen table and was careful not to get them messed up.

To Winnipeg - 1950

We moved to Winnipeg from northern Saskatchewan when I was nine. Daddy had gone ahead of us, and Mommy and me and Petey and Polly had been living with Babba and Dedda in Yorkton for a few months. I finished grade three in Yorkton. When we left for Winnipeg, we rode on the train for most of the day. Uncle Walter picked us up downtown at the railway station. We had been on train trips before, and I had been in cities in Saskatchewan, like Nipawin and Prince Albert and Yorkton, but it just seemed so very crowded and busy on the streets of Winnipeg. It was early July, so the late afternoon was still full of sunshine. And the streets were full of people. And of noise.

I watched so many people walking up and down the sidewalks on both sides of the street. The roads were made out of cement, and so were the sidewalks. Uncle Walter told us that the street was called Portage Avenue, and it was the main street of the city. The sun flashed off the windows of some of the very tall buildings along both sides of the street. I counted six stories in one of them. Right next to the sidewalk there were rows of stores. Some of them looked like Daddy's store in Garrick, but many of them had bigger windows and signs and even lights on in the middle of a sunny afternoon. I saw restaurants, stores with ladies' dresses in the windows, one with a big red sign talking about insurance and another one saying that you could find a dentist upstairs. There were so many streets, and I was being absorbed by all this action and rushing.

Then, as Uncle Walter drove along, I noticed the lights on the street corners. When they were red, he stopped the car. And the other cars beside us stopped too. But not all the cars on the streets stopped. Some of them drove past in front of us after we stopped. Then the funny lights turned green, and my uncle's car and the cars beside us started driving again. What was going on? I became fascinated by those changing red and green lights. Soon I noticed that there were not as many cars on some streets, but Uncle Walter and the other cars stopped anyway when the light was red.

I finally said to Uncle Walter, "Why do they have those red and green lights?" He started to laugh, but then he told me that the red light meant that he and all the cars beside him had to stop, so that the cars going the other way could go past in front of him. Then, when the light turned green, he and the cars beside him could go ahead. They took turns.

"But why can't you just look and see if nobody is coming? Then you could go ahead without all these red and green lights."

He just laughed even harder, and said, "Winnipeg is a big city, Ruthie."

That answer didn't help me much. By then we were turning onto a bigger, wider street. We crossed a bridge over a river, we saw more streets filled with stores, but not so many tall buildings.

I listened to Mommy talking to her brother about where we would all be sleeping that night and when could she talk to Mrs. Anderson. Babba and Dedda had already moved into a new house that Dedda had built in Winnipeg. Until our new house down the same street was finished, we would be renting the house next door from a lady named Mrs. Anderson, who was going to visit her family in another town for the summer.

We drove out along another wide street with not so many tall buildings and some spaces that were only empty fields full of tall grass. Mommy told me that this was called Pembina Highway. It would take us to Fort Garry, the name of the part of Winnipeg where we would be living.

Uncle Walter was now an architect, and he was telling my Mommy about designing houses in a style that suited the modern times we were living in. As the only boy in Babba and Dedda's family, he had been sent to university to study architecture, and then he began working with Dedda designing homes. He was also a partner in a firm of architects, something my grandparents were very, very proud of.

Finally we turned off the highway onto our street. Well, the corner almost looked to me as if I was still back home. On one side was a grocery store, something like Daddy's store in Garrick, with steps leading up to the front door with a big window on each side of the door. A sign on the front said "Chesney's Grocery" in bright red letters.

Maybe I was going to like this Winnipeg.

Printed in Canada